Forgiveness and Politics

Praise for Forgiveness and Politics

Forgiveness and Politics *sounds like an unlikely combination of subjects but they are ever more relevant in trying to untangle and resolve entrenched impasses like the Naga Political Issue. This complex problem lies at the heart of ethnic Asia long before there ever was an independent India or Burma, later Myanmar. The work is the result of deep inner urgings and enriched by the personal experiences in the author's own family.*

Forgiveness and Politics, *initially a monograph, won the Gordon Graham Prize for Naga Literature (GGPNL) in the non-fiction category in 2018-19. The work was first narrowed down by a team of international jurists and finally selected as the winner by a panel of eminent judges in India. A must read for any student of Conflict Resolution.*

Charles Chasie, Author and President, Kohima Educational Society
(Partner organisation of the KET, UK, & organisers of the GGPNL)

I found Forgiveness and Politics *to be quite an exceptional book because of its scope and treatment of a topic which has great relevance to the present socio-political situation in Nagaland. The author's deep knowledge of the Biblical texts and the way he connects them with the main corpus of the book, which takes up the theme of forgiveness and politics, is indeed commendable. This is a deeply introspective book where the realities of the Naga situation find a place within the interwoven fabric of religious and political theories which leave the impression that the search for a satisfactory solution would involve a movement towards reconciliation not only among the participants of the Naga struggle but also those who are outside its parameters.*

Professor Udayon Misra, Former Head of English,
Dibrugarh University, and a National Fellow of the
Indian Council of Social Science Research and of the
Indian Institute of Advanced Study

Kethoser Kevichusa's Forgiveness and Politics *is based on a radical understanding of the intrinsic relation between forgiveness and politics — that politics itself is an inherently forgiving enterprise. The author is committed to acute observation and engagement with the idea of forgiveness and politics and their profound relationship with justice and reconciliation but one that is not divorced from the realities on the ground. Drawing on the experiences of the Northern Ireland conflict and the role of forgiveness there, he offers thoughtful proposals for the possibility of peace and reconciliation in the political conflict of his own deeply divided land. This commitment to the healing power of forgiveness as an agent of social change is moving and inspiring. Firmly Christian in perspective, Kevichusa grounds his arguments in the metanarrative of Scripture and connects biblical text with the main corpus of the book in a way that is both uncanny and marvellous. Truthful and hopeful, this work offers its readers a spiritual release that they might not have realised they were looking for.*

Dr. Kevileno Sakhrie
(Retd. Associate Professor, Kohima College, Nagaland)

It has been a privilege to have been asked to abridge the work that Aniu Kevichusa did for his doctorate at the Oxford Centre for Mission Studies into this shorter version which we hope will gain a wide readership. His work on forgiveness and politics comes out of his personal experience in Nagaland which includes the murder of some of his family members. He compares the situation there with the conflict in Northern Ireland and his explanation of the background to that situation is the most informative account that I have seen. In reflecting what the Bible says in relation to forgiveness and relating it to justice and reconciliation within the political sphere, he describes a story that has relevance far beyond the shores of India and Northern Ireland to many other situations in the world today.

Professor David Cranston D.Phil FRCS, Chairman of the Board of the Oxford Centre for Mission Studies

Forgiveness and Politics

A Critical Appraisal

Kethoser Aniu Kevichusa

regnum

First published 2021 by Regnum Books International

This book was abridged by David Cranston.

Regnum is an imprint of the Oxford Centre for Mission Studies
St. Philip and St. James Church
Woodstock Road, Oxford OX2 6HR, UK
www.ocms.ac.uk/regnum

British Library Cataloguing in Publication Data. A catalogue record for this book is available from the British Library.

ISBN: 978-1-5064-8366-5

eBook ISBN: 978-1-5064-8388-7

Typeset in Candara by Words by Design.

Photo by Joel Filipe on www.unsplash.com

The publication of this volume is made possible through the financial assistance of Evangelisches Missionswerk.

Distributed by Fortress Press in the US, Canada, India, and Brazil

Contents

Introduction

From my earliest years, I knew that forgiveness makes a difference; forgiveness often saved me from my parents' stick! I knew that their forgiving my childhood faults, both trivial and serious, invariably led to the restoration of our relationship. I also knew grew up knowing both that God forgave people their sins in and because of Jesus Christ, and that Christians are required to forgive others. When I put my trust in Christ as a teenager, I also experienced the sense of freedom, joy, and peace that comes from the knowledge of sins forgiven. I thus grew up learning, practising, and receiving forgiveness.

However, while there was no doubt in my mind that forgiveness makes a difference in interpersonal relationships and divine-human relationships, I began to wonder if it had any power in the wider world of politics and political conflict. In 1956, my maternal grandfather was murdered by a Naga nationalist group fighting for Naga independence from India. In 1992 and 1996, two of my paternal uncles, both Naga political leaders and brothers, were assassinated by another nationalist group. During the funerals of these two uncles, my father, as head of the Kevichusa family clan, declared that our family forgave the murderers, and that the family would not harbour any intention of revenge. However, none of those involved in the murders have been brought to justice and there has not been any reconciliation. I have since often wondered how forgiveness and politics are related, and how forgiveness might have a role in the mitigation or resolution of the Naga political conflict. While my exploration has its roots in my own family experience, I have always wanted to think more theologically, philosophically, and ethically around the relations between forgiveness and politics.

With this in mind, this book, a précis of my doctorate, has looked in depth at two areas of conflict: Northern Ireland and the resulting Good Friday Agreement and the Naga political conflict. It explores how forgiveness might have political import in breaking the cycles of violence and conflict in Ireland and Nagaland.

Nagas are a hill people comprising several tribes, spread over India's north-eastern states of Nagaland, Assam, Arunachal Pradesh, Manipur, and parts of north-western Myanmar. For over six decades, the Nagas have been embroiled in one of the world's longest, but little-known conflicts, which originally began as a struggle for Naga independence but has long since degenerated into a cycle of inter-factional feuds that has caught Naga society in the vortex of hatred, violence, and vengeance. About 90 per cent of Nagas are Christians, predominantly Baptists. Christianity in Nagaland contributes significantly to the way Nagas interpret and respond to the world and the predominance of Christianity also means that its resources, not least the concept of forgiveness, can be tapped into in the search for peace and reconciliation in the Naga situation.

I have also chosen the Northern Irish conflict as a comparison. Although in many ways very different from the Naga conflict, it seemed to be an appropriate choice because the geographical size and population are roughly the same of both regions; the religious context is predominantly Christian; the political conflicts are both fuelled by nationalistic aspirations, and most of the questions being asked regarding forgiveness are similar. What transpired during the peace process that culminated in the 1998 Good Friday Agreement can be understood as a form of forgiveness in politics. Understanding this makes an original contribution to the existing body of literature on forgiveness in the Northern Irish conflict, illustrates the theoretical argument of forgiveness in politics, and offers a model for the resolution of the Naga conflict.

The Biblical Foundations of Forgiveness

Introduction

Forgiveness is a distinctly Christian ethic, as affirmed in the Bible. In seeking the biblical foundations for forgiveness, a number of approaches have been taken: *the philological, the precepts, the principles,* and *the paradigms.* While these approaches are not mutually exclusive, distinguishing between them is helpful.

The philological approach is dependent on the study of the biblical words for forgiveness. For instance, a study of the New Testament Greek word, *aphiemi* (lit. "to let go," and usually translated "to forgive"), comprises two complementary strands, both the act of letting go of hatred and seeking the good of another.

The precepts approach to forgiveness is conditional upon repentance and confession, but raises questions as to whether divine forgiveness is conditional upon human forgiveness, and whether one can 'take revenge *after* forgiving seventy times seven and... hit back after having turned the other cheek.'

The principles approach takes the view that the Bible is a book which contains principles of moral behaviour and human conduct and what really matters is the principle behind the text, "the timeless kernel behind the cultural husk."[1]

The paradigms approach roots Christian ethics on stories or characters in the Bible that give good or bad examples of faith and obedience. Hence, the actions of persons or groups are to be judged morally wrong if they are judged to be wrong under similar circumstances as those found in Scripture.

Yet these approaches ignore the metanarrative of the Bible which places these moral bricks within the grand story of the *whole* biblical metanarrative.

The Story of the Bible

In the last two decades, N. T. Wright has become one of the most influential biblical scholars understanding the Bible as a grand story, suggesting five acts:[2]

Act I	*Creation*
Act II	*Fall*
Act III	*Israel*
Act IV	*Jesus*
Act V	*Church*

Within this scheme, Wright suggests that the present church *continues* to live in the fifth act. This act opens with Easter and Pentecost, and the apostolic period forms the first scene of the fifth act.

However, others argue that this particular model is mistaken in that it puts the church at the end of the story; rather the story begins and ends with God. Taking on board some of those criticisms, while still remaining in fundamental agreement with Wright, another model may be proposed:

The Biblical Story: A Proposed Model

Act I (Exposition)	*Creation*
Scene 1	*Creation*
Scene 2	*Fall*
Act II (Rising Action)	*Covenant*
Act III (Climax)	*Christ: The Beginning of New Creation*
Act IV (Falling Action)	*Church*
Scene 1	*The New Testament Church*
Scene 2	*The Church since the NT Church*
Act V (Dénouement)	*Consummation:* *The Completion of New Creation*

The strength of this model is that it remains simple, with a symmetry that corresponds not only with the biblical story but also with a classical dramatic structure. It also has the crucial connection between Act III and Act V: "Jesus: The *Beginning* of New Creation," and "Consummation: The *Completion* of New Creation".

What has all this got to do with forgiveness?

Forgiveness and "Creation"

Forgiveness is both a divine response and a human response and is the operative principle that undergirds God's relation and engagement with the world. It is forgiveness that is behind God's creation, sustenance, redemption, and consummation of creation. To that extent, it is forgiveness that gives meaning to the understanding of God as Creator, Sustainer, and Redeemer. God made the world and he made it good and therefore no matter how fallen, it cannot be allowed to founder in ultimate futility. It is also only through such an understanding of God's forgiveness that one can make sense of difficult passages such as Hebrews 19:26, 1 Peter 1:20, and Revelation 13:8, which appear to suggest Christ's destiny as God's lamb slain "before the foundation of the world." These passages hint that forgiveness is built into the very core of God's act of creation, and are manifested in his subsequent works of sustenance, redemption, and consummation. Forgiveness is foundational to God's relation with the world.

Forgiveness is thus the most appropriate roadmap for negotiating a journey through life in the world. The biblical metanarrative begins with Creation, recognising that there *is* a created reality and order. It is an ethic which assumes a good, divinely ordained moral order that governs relations among God's creatures, but there has been a disruption in the natural and moral order because of the fall. The fall affects ourselves as well as others. All stand as sinners in equal need of forgiveness before God and create an empathy that, according to the Scriptures, makes forgiveness an obligation and a duty (cf. Mt. 18:23-35).

Forgiveness does not mean sins against oneself do not matter. They do matter, otherwise there would not be anything to forgive. Forgiveness judges – albeit with empathy, humility, and charity – certain actions as wrong and the state of affairs arising thereby as unacceptable. Judgement and condemnation are intrinsic to forgiveness, but forgiveness is not just about judging and condemning wrongdoing, it is also about redeeming wrongdoing, predicated on the fact that the world is itself redeemed in Christ. The present world is not a world without sin, but neither is it a world without redemption. This leads to the question of how forgiveness relates to the notion of "New Creation."

Forgiveness and "Covenant"

The story of Israel, begins on the heels of the world that has gone wrong, with the promise that the earth would be blessed through Israel (Gen. 1-11; Gen. 12:1-3; Gen. 17). At the heart of Israel and Judaism is the covenant, unilateral, not bilateral and established by YHWH, to be unconditionally faithful to Israel. Israel did not initiate, or merit God's faithfulness and commitment to it, but it was costly in terms of the obligations it placed upon Israel, summarised in the Ten Commandments. Far from playing down Israel's response, it placed Israel under the free obligation to respond faithfully. The indicatives of grace, the affirmations of God's unconditional covenant commitment and faithfulness precede the imperatives of law, they do not follow it.

It is this unconditional love and forgiveness of God towards a sinful, rebellious, and confused humanity that stands at the heart of the Christian faith. The Christian conception of repentance, denotes the transformation that emerges from an appreciation of unconditional grace. Thus, repentance can also be understood as taking place after forgiveness, and the result is peace and reconciliation – *shalom*. The duty of human forgiveness is a natural, not a coerced, response to God's unconditional love and grace.

To speak of Israel's *appropriate* response of faithfulness and obedience to God's unconditional commitment and faithfulness is one thing, but to speak of Israel's *actual* faithfulness and obedience is another. The defeat and subjugation of the Jewish nation by pagans and the destruction and desecration of the temple were symbolic of God's giving over of Israel to the consequences of their sin and disobedience. The one word for all this was *Exile*. NT Wright points out that, as long as the Jews remained in exile (specifically in Babylon), they *knew* that their sins had not been forgiven. To be in exile, for the Jews, was to be "un-forgiven," and to return from exile was to be forgiven.

Israel's return from exile was, however, not an end in itself. The biblical story points to the plan of God that it was to be through Israel that the world would be redeemed. Furthermore, the restoration of Israel would include not only the salvation of the Gentiles, but also the renewal of the whole of creation. And it is here that Jesus (in Act III) takes the stage.

Forgiveness and "Christ"

To the earliest Christians, the resurrection proved that Jesus was Israel's long-awaited Davidic Messiah, who brought about the true end of exile. Through his life, death, and resurrection, he defeated the enemies of the people of God, rebuilt the temple, and brought about the God-given reign of righteousness and peace. It is in the person and work of Jesus Christ that God's forgiveness is enacted, and Old Testament passages show the connection between the resurrection of Jesus, the return from exile, and forgiveness as in Hosea 6:1-2:

"Come, and let us return to the LORD; it is he who has torn, and he will heal us; he has struck down, and he will bind us up. *After two days he will revive us; on the third day he will raise us up, that we may live before him.*"

Once Israel was restored, the world itself was renewed. The resurrection of Jesus meant not only Israel's return from exile, but also the beginning of the new creation. Of all the biblical books, the understanding of the resurrection as the beginning of new creation is most elegantly portrayed in the book of John. The very first phrase of the Gospel, "In the beginning" itself evoking creation imagery, the theme of new creation becomes profound on Good Friday, the sixth day, when, just as in the first creation account, the initial work of new creation culminates with the true human to whom the attention of the world is summoned: "Behold, the Man!" (Jn. 19:5). This is followed by the great shout of completion, "It is finished!" (Jn. 19:30). The new humanity, created in Christ, is also proleptically breathed into with the Holy Spirit and is commissioned to undertake new tasks (Jn. 20:22-23).

Forgiveness and "Church"

According to the model offered, the vocation of the church is about living as a "resurrection community" and living in the "forgiven-ness" and "forgiving-ness" of new creation.

The call of Christ to the new community is to embody forgiveness which comes alive in Jesus' command to forgive "not seven times, but seventy times seven" (Mt. 18:22) and this command can also be understood as an echo of the Jubilee Year commandment of the Old Testament. The same command for forgiveness is also symbolic of the inauguration of the new age in Jesus. It is only through forgiveness that sin, rebellion, and wrongdoing are covered and brought to an end, and true justice and righteousness are brought about. The vocation of the church is to embody forgiveness and witness to its power.

Forgiveness and "Consummation"

The new creation will be consummated in the eschaton, the final event of the Divine plan (Act V), and the new creation that is inaugurated in the person and work of Christ is not "a *mere* restoration, the return of the *status quo ante*,"[3] but a movement towards the renewal of all things. Christians, along with everyone else, must remain agnostic as to *how* and *when* the final new creation will *come*. The end of the story is in the hands of God.

There are a number of implications that these truths have for a biblical understanding of forgiveness. First of all, forgiveness is the core of the new creation. It is a response to the biblical summons to live in God's new world. For the philosopher Kierkegaard, if creation miraculously brings being out of nothing and turns absence into a presence, forgiveness, equally miraculously, de-creates, and turns what is into what is not. In the Bible, the final new creation is not just about the incorporation of *saintly* human history and *saintly* human works, but of *sinful* human history and *sinful* human works. Like the new creation itself, forgiveness involves both continuity and discontinuity with the past. In the resurrection of Jesus, there is both continuity and discontinuity. The body of Jesus was a transformed and glorified body, no longer bound by the limitations of time and space. The hermeneutical tension between the "already" and the "not yet" is a recognised characteristic of New Testament ethics itself.

Oliver O'Donovan, former Regius Professor of Moral and Pastoral Theology at the University of Oxford, says that "to forgive will always be a matter of limping painfully after."[4] Forgiveness, as a truly biblical ethic, must be grounded in the metanarrative of Scripture that spans from creation to the new creation. It is a matter of living faithfully, and realistically, in "the time between the times." Forgiveness can then be understood not merely as a religious, an intra-personal, or an inter-personal practice. It can also be a truly political practice. And it is to the question of forgiveness as a political practice that this book will now turn.

Forgiveness and Politics

There are a number of objections to mixing forgiveness and politics. In the interpersonal realm, the perspective over an issue is often limited to that of the wrongdoer and the wronged, while in the public realm, perspectives are multiplied due to the number of parties involved. However, interpersonal contexts are also complex. For example, adultery is not simply an interpersonal wrong between two spouses, for children and other family members are also involved. Therefore, if the complexity of interests disqualifies forgiveness from entering the political realm, it should also be disqualified in the personal realm.

Another objection is that the offer of apology or forgiveness at the political level brings with it the risk of unpredictable consequences. For example, if one is forgiven by another for stealing a laptop computer, the stolen laptop should still be returned. The restitution may be waived, or the restitution may be impossible if, for example, the laptop is broken or sold – but the liability of restitution remains. Jesus himself did not object to Zacchaeus's resolution for a fourfold restitution (cf. Lk. 19:1-10).

Furthermore, political apologies are typically made by persons not responsible, on behalf of those who were, but this also happens in personal contexts, not detracting from the apology. For instance, as the father of young children, I may apologise to a neighbour whose windowpanes were broken by my children throwing stones at them.

Forgiveness and Politics: A Proposal

The first and most famous use of the word "politics" is found in Aristotle's *Politics,* and is that special kind of human relationship that arises in the city (*polis*), and the nature of rule that is best for it. The political method of establishing order is different from any other method, for it does not seek to do it by coercion or violence, as a tyrant might. For Aristotle, a tyrant who uses coercion or violence to enforce order is not involved in politics.

Haddon Willmer, Emeritus Professor of Theology at Leeds University, uses the phrase, "the politics of forgiveness."[5] He suggests that one must begin by looking for the presence of forgiveness in politics, rather than its absence. His contention is that, without forgiveness operating in any society, people cannot live together with the degree of amicableness and cooperation that is commonly present. Forgiveness in politics is not so much an *ought* as it is an *is.* It is at work in the political realm, more than expected or anticipated, and is indispensable to the existence of civil society.

Politics arises from the acceptance of the fact that there exists within a specific territorial unit of common rule, different groups with different traditions and conflicting agendas. The political method of rule is to listen to these groups and conciliate them as far as possible, giving them a sense of security, and a safe means of articulation by which they can speak freely.

If one subscribes to a conception of politics that embraces conciliation and compromise, then one begins to appreciate the relationship between politics and forgiveness. Indeed, it could even be claimed that forgiveness is the *sine qua non* of politics. It is a forgiving spirit that makes politics possible and creates the space to engage in politics instead of war.

Dialogue, Compromise, Realism, Reconciliation, and Forgiveness

Dialogue is one of the most important elements of the political method. Forgiveness works through a dialogue between the wrongdoer and the wronged, with the wrongdoer expressing remorse for the wrong done, and the wronged granting forgiveness. Dialogue is based on the principles of equality and reciprocity which allow the parties to interact as equals. Forgiveness and dialogue both require a commitment to treat a person as a human being, with respect and dignity, even if one disapproves of their actions or disagrees with their views.

Empathy is another important element of forgiveness. To empathise in a process of dialogue is about being sensitive to the feelings of the other, not necessarily agreeing with them. It is also about being conscious that one's own views and opinions might be fallible and open to correction.

However political conflicts are often so deeply embedded in moral categories of right and wrong that making compromises is perceived to be tantamount to lowering one's ethical and moral ideals. One way of dealing with this is to differentiate between *political* and *ethical* problems, although this can be artificial. Political deliberations have ethical dimensions, just as ethical deliberations have political implications; to that extent, if politics has to make compromises, so too does ethics. Very often, the *right* thing to do in life is to compromise, while the *wrong* thing to do is to insist on fully realising one's ethical insights or theological convictions.

The vocation of politics, like that of philosophy, requires a creative blend of commitment to particular positions and tolerance of opposing positions. It is in this creative blend that politicians find their identity and retain their integrity in the midst of compromise. Political compromise is often necessary, not because politicians give up their personal convictions over a certain issue, but because they understand their vocation as politicians to help create conditions under which *all*, including those with whom they disagree, can live with dignity and freedom. In that sense, there is a difference between what one regards as an individual as a morally correct course of action, and what one regards as a politician in a diverse and pluralistic society, as the politically correct course of action.

Forgiveness makes it possible to believe in "absolute" morality on the one hand, while at the same time engaging with the imperfect reality of things. It is only through forgiveness that the interface between the tensile poles of imperfect society and absolute morality becomes possible. A central function of politics is to create and safeguard a space where different and conflicting views are heard, safeguarding the possibility of reconciliation.

Such an approach, because of its understanding of politics as distinct from war, seems to be the only approach that can meaningfully talk of forgiveness *in the midst* of conflict. All other accounts talk of forgiveness only in a post-conflict scenario, and to that extent, provide little or no resources for *ending* violence and war. This approach, however, an understanding of politics as a forgiving enterprise, and its vocation as community-building and reconciliation-seeking, could be another way of ending war and violence. It provides an understanding of forgiveness that is about breaking the cycle of violence, rather than one that is meaningful only after the violence has ended.

Forgiveness and Justice

Introduction

Perhaps the biggest objection against incorporating forgiveness into politics is the feeling that forgiveness can undermine justice. This stems from the assumption that forgiveness and justice, are opposite responses to wrongdoing.

It is true that forgiveness presupposes an initial wrongdoing or injustice. Without such an injustice, forgiveness would be unnecessary. However, if that initial injustice is not addressed, it often leads to unforgiveness or even revenge. Revenge is closely tied to the failure of dispensing justice. O'Donovan says, "Built into the human nature that we share, is an elemental thirst for justice, which, when human law and order breaks down, reasserts itself in this most terrible form."[6] Desire for, or acts of, revenge reflect human nature's innate thirst for justice, and relate to legitimate concerns for taking evil seriously.

In most Western conceptions and systems of justice and forgiveness, justice is primarily operative in the impersonal sphere as part of the social glue that binds a society together, dealing with the legal side of wrongdoing. Forgiveness is primarily operative in the personal or relational sphere dealing with the moral side of wrongdoing. Individuals or persons in their personal and private capacities forgive, but institutions or states in their public duties, capacities and functions will seek justice.

However, such conceptions and systems of justice could be criticised for not giving enough attention to the relational aspects of crime. The dichotomy of justice and forgiveness reflects too high a view of justice and too low an understanding of forgiveness, and the dichotomy tends to remove forgiveness from the whole realm of human relations. However, the growing popularity of "restorative justice" and "political forgiveness", and the effectiveness of quasi-judicial commissions on truth and reconciliation speak of the growing awareness that forgiveness and justice must be incorporated.

The common understanding among many people, including Christians, is that "There is no forgiveness without repentance and confession." Such an understanding of forgiveness makes it difficult for many Christians to engage in processes of forgiveness in the absence of justice. A conditional understanding of forgiveness is not unique to Christians, many argue that justice is a precondition for forgiveness; that there is no forgiveness without justice.

Is this true? An argument which places justice as a precondition for forgiveness is problematic on several counts for it goes against the grain of forgiveness as a free, unconditional, and gracious act. If repentance and restitution are forthcoming, all well and good, but forgiveness cannot be dependent on these. Such an account makes forgiveness more or less redundant. It would be quite meaningless, to claim that a debtor has been forgiven their debt after they have paid it all off, or that a wrongdoer is forgiven of their wrong after they have been punished fully for their wrongdoing. Moreover, it can also be argued that societies that have properly functioning judicial systems, such as in the West, tend to be less forgiving. A fixation on justice often betrays an unforgiving spirit. Justice often feeds on unforgiveness.

Moreover, in a world rife with conflict, a fixation on the ideal of justice can be quite dangerous, because it can be blind to the limitation of justice. First of all, agreements on the nature of justice are hard to come by, begging the question, "Whose justice?" This is evident in many conflict-torn situations, where there is a volatile mix of governments and a confusing assortment of "laws". What is murder according to one family or group can be considered capital punishment, passed by the court of another government, for treason in the name of justice.

Writing from the context of the Northern Ireland conflict, Kevin O'Higgins, who was a judge of the High Court in Northern Ireland, gives two reasons why justice, even when dispensed properly by law courts, is often unsatisfactory to people.[7] First, he says, in addition to natural feelings of anger, failure, sadness, and anxiety caused by wrongdoing, court proceedings are often a source of considerable stress, even when there are sufficient financial assets to meet the judicial processes. Second, even if cases where verdicts are given to the relative satisfaction of the parties, many of those involved, especially litigants, leave court with a feeling that they have not had an opportunity to articulate the sense of hurt and wrong that they have experienced and that their sense of grievance has been ignored. Perfect justice will always remain an elusive quest. Even the best of human societies remain only "nearly just." "Final justice" is the prerogative of God.

The third limitation of retributive justice has to do with human limitation. As O'Donovan puts it, "Justice is a good for which man has an infinite desire but a limited capacity."[8] Relentless pursuit of justice makes life unliveable and social coexistence impossible. In real life, nobody can go around society and through life condemning and punishing every wrongdoing they encounter. Failure to condemn or punish all the wrongs that one comes across may not amount to condonation, but one often does not do it simply because it would take too much of our time and sour all our relationships.

Furthermore, an infinite human desire for justice is not matched by a corresponding capacity of humans for discrimination and insight. The closer we get, the more the line between the guilty and innocent blurs and we see an intractable maze of small and large hatreds, dishonesties, manipulations, and brutalities, each reinforcing the other. This is, of course, not to deny that victims and their families have been violated. But it is to point out that, in cases of conflicts, the "knotted histories" of individuals and groups make the disentangling of the innocent from the blameworthy and the drawing of lines in terms of clear and distinct mappings of good and evil, just and unjust, and victims and victimisers overwhelmingly more complex than they initially appear.

A third implication is that in many situations, individuals or communities who seek to make judgements are themselves often not just enough. Commenting on the story of Jesus and the woman caught in adultery (Jn. 8:3-11), O'Donovan says:

> *Jesus does not challenge the generic categories in which the judges describe the act, nor does he challenge the application of those categories to the accused woman. But he demands that another dimension of description should be included: the ambiguous relation in which those who accuse others of adultery stand to the adulterers. And so he challenges the discrimination they have made. Were that community to carry out the death penalty on that woman, the line between innocence and guilty would have been wrongly drawn.*[9]

O'Donovan's point is that it is only when the dimension of the truth of the community that seeks to judge is taken into consideration that a satisfactory discrimination between the innocent and the guilty can be given. It is only by taking into consideration the truth of the community that judges and condemns, the ambiguity of their own moral status and the ambivalence of the relation in which they stand with those they judge, that discrimination between the innocent and the guilty can be made. However, communities of judgment often fail to do that in their search for justice, and their judgments and condemnations become unjust in the process.

Justice and Forgiveness, Even Forgiveness First

In recent years, proposals to overcome the deadlock that arises from a "justice first" approach have been made by recasting the relation between forgiveness and justice. One way is by arguing that forgiveness complements justice. This approach finds its most powerful and authoritative voice in Pope John Paul II's message *No*

Peace without Justice, No Justice without Forgiveness. On 1 January 2002, speaking on the heels of 9/11, Pope John Paul II, in his World Day of Peace message, carried forth the tradition of his predecessors in calling justice a pillar of peace. He went on to say, "But because human justice is always fragile and imperfect, subject as it is to the limitations and egoism of individuals and groups, it must include and be completed by the *forgiveness which heals and rebuilds troubled human relations from their foundations.*"[10]

Situating the search for justice within the larger framework of forgiveness and reconciliation relaxes the tension between forgiveness and justice. However, there is another way of relaxing the tension between justice and forgiveness, by revisiting the concept of justice itself.

Revisiting Justice

Martha Nussbaum, an American philosopher and Professor of Law and Ethics at the University of Chicago, identifies how two ideas of retributive justice emerged over time by examining justice as *dikê* and *epieikeia*.[11]

Dikê, on the one hand, is about paying back in kind, so retribution must be proportional to the original encroachment. It pays no attention to the particular circumstances under which an initial wrong was committed and is always harsh and unyielding. Sometimes the harshness is merited, sometimes it is excessive. But it is rarely too soft, for it begins from the assumption that the doer should suffer.

On the other hand, there emerged in ancient thought, particularly through Aristotle, the idea of justice as *epieikeia* (equity). *Epieikeia* sought to pay attention to the particular circumstances of a certain wrong and determined punishment by taking those particulars into account.

For Aristotle, *epieikeia* judges with the wrongdoer and hears their side of the story; tries to see things from that person's point of view, to comprehend the obstacles that the wrongdoer faced when they acted.

When justice is understood and approached as *epieikeia,* then forgiveness and justice need not be seen as two diametrically opposed concepts and practices, where one is dispensed at the expense of the other. Justice itself, as it "bends" to consider the particularities of each case, bends towards forgiveness. *Epieikeia* is also alert to the fact of "cultural sin" and "structural violence," whereby wrongdoers are themselves victims of historical fate and accidents. *Epieikeia* questions whether what often passes as "justice" may sometimes be revenge in the guise of justice, and whether a relentless pursuit of rigid justice as *dikê* endangers one's own well-being and that of society.

Punishment is not in conflict with forgiveness. There can be both forgiveness and punishment. Forgiveness can also call for the protection of innocents through punishment that disables the wrongdoer so that they can injure no more. Forgiveness would also seek the instruction and discipline of the wrongdoer, if necessary through punishment, for the good of the wrongdoers themselves. Finally, forgiveness will also strive for the reception of the wrongdoer into the community in reconciliation. It is this relation between reconciliation and forgiveness that the next chapter considers.

Forgiveness and Reconciliation

The word *reconciliation* comes from the Latin word *concilium*, meaning a deliberative process "in council" for working out differences among adversaries. In the Old Testament, reconciliation is closely linked to the concept of *shalom*, meaning peace, understood not simply as the absence of violence but the realisation of justice and mutual love, promoting one another's good. In Hebrew, the phrase *tikkun olam* means "to heal, to transform" or, more broadly, "to repair the world." For the Apostle Paul, reconciliation has to do with the overcoming of enmity between God and creation, and the restoration of peaceful relations on the basis of the work of Christ.

For Christians, all human processes of reconciliation have their sights fixed on the perfect state of reconciliation promised only in the eschaton. It is impossible to talk of a state of reconciliation without a process of reconciliation. Even reconciliation as a state of resignation to one's circumstances always involves a *process* of reconciliation *with* one's circumstances.

In recent decades, particularly following the South African experience, reconciliation has become a familiar political concept, and the English term "reconciliation" has gained almost universal parlance. In political discourse, it is used loosely to imply a setting aside of past animosities and the possibility of former enemies working together in the future.

According to the New Testament, reconciliation is not limited exclusively to persons, whether God with humans, or humans with humans: "God was in Christ," the Apostle Paul says, "reconciling the world to himself" (2 Cor. 5:19). The purpose of God is, through Christ, "to reconcile to himself all things, whether things on earth or things in heaven" (Col. 1:20). The reconciliation between God and humanity is but a part of the reconciliation between God and creation.

To reconcile problems is about finding workable, if imperfect, solutions to difficulties. It is about easing, not erasing, existing tensions. Similarly, to be reconciled to certain realities is about accepting and learning to live with them with hopeful forbearance that they are somehow acceptable. For Christians, learning to be reconciled on this side of eternity is about learning to live with the imperfection of humanity and reality.

Forgiveness can be unilateral and unconditional; but reconciliation is almost always mutual and conditional. One can forgive another, but when the other refuses to acknowledge the wrong done, the two cannot be reconciled in the truest sense of the word. In such cases, the victim has *forgiven* but the wrongdoer has not *received* the victim's forgiveness, which would have resulted in reconciliation. It is thus possible for there to be forgiveness without reconciliation, even if there can be no reconciliation without forgiveness. Forgiveness *seeks, hopes* – and *prays – for* reconciliation. Forgiveness leaves the door open for reconciliation. Reconciliation is the end of a process that forgiveness begins.

Forgiveness can thus contribute significantly to the reconciliation of a society; indeed, forgiveness is indispensable in approaching the question of reconciliation in conflict situations and can be illustrated through the following two diagrams.

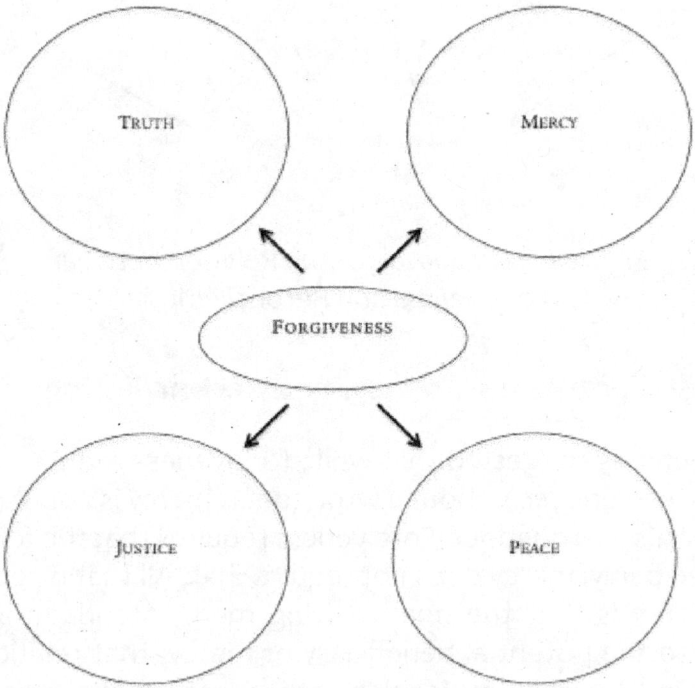

Figure A: The Relation of Forgiveness to Truth, Mercy, Justice, and Peace

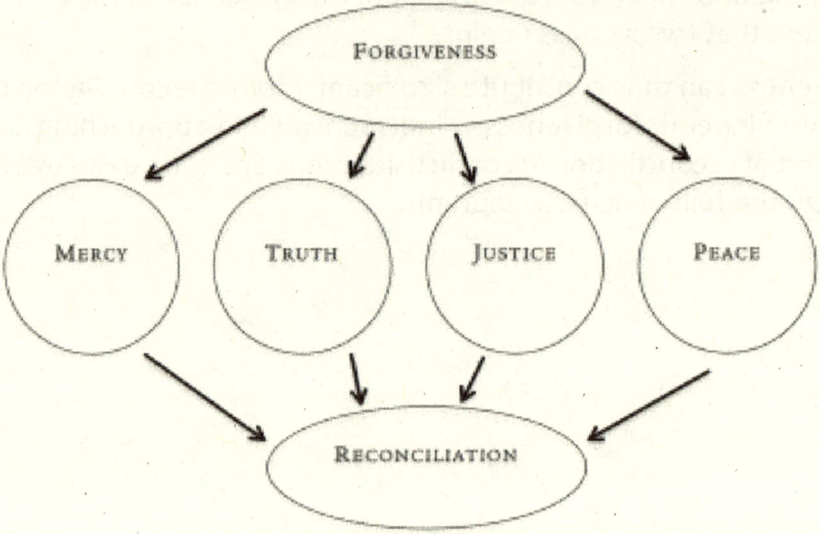

Figure B: A Proposal for the Relation between Forgiveness and Reconciliation

Forgiveness, Mercy, and Reconciliation

It is sometimes suggested that while forgiveness requires that one changes how one *feels* about a wrongdoer, mercy is about how one *acts* towards a wrongdoer. Forgiveness requires that the forgiver be an injured party, mercy does not require that. All that is required to show mercy is that the one showing mercy stands in a certain relation to the potential beneficiary of mercy; that relation being establishing typically by legal or other institutional rules. While forgiveness flows from internal emotional transformation, mercy is an external gift to a wrongdoer. To that extent, one can forgive without showing mercy, and can show mercy, even begrudgingly, without forgiving. Thus, some argue that non-human entities (such as the state or the judicial system), by virtue of their incapacity of feeling moral emotions, cannot forgive; they can only show mercy. However, in many cases of wrongdoing, there are direct and indirect victims. This, in turn, means that indirect injured parties, including the state, can also forgive. All cases of mercy presuppose an injury, direct or indirect, against the one granting mercy. To that extent, the alleged difference between forgiveness and mercy collapses.

A person who forgives and, at the same time, fails to show mercy takes with one hand what is given by the other. Thus, forgiveness and mercy have similar qualities, and each concept contains the other as a constituent element.

Forgiveness, Peace, and Reconciliation

On the face of it, it should not be too problematic to claim that forgiveness and peace are related, just as peace and reconciliation are related. But, as is often the case, peace, understood as the end or absence of conflict, can also be achieved through other means: by using force through victory and subjugation, through a suspension of hostile activities or through the separation of the conflicting parties. And yet, peace achieved through these means can often leave resentment and hostility brewing underneath, preparing the way for more deadly future conflicts. The achievement of peace through the separation of conflicting groups does little to lead to reconciliation, as is evident in cases such as the creation of the modern state of Israel (through the separation of Jews and Europeans after World War II), the partition of British India into India and Pakistan, or the partition of Ireland.

Reconciliation requires more, not less, than peace. However, if peace is to have a better chance of leading to reconciliation, then there must be forgiveness, for without forgiveness, there can be no real peace and no lasting reconciliation. If societies are to move beyond the mere ending of conflict, if they are to move beyond peace to reconciliation, then forgiveness is the more *hopeful* path. As Willmer puts it:

> *Forgiveness is a word which points to a more hopeful end to conflict than oppressive or pyrrhic victory, the merely temporary suspension of hostility or the separation of combatants. It implies living together rather than living apart. It is a sign that there are resources for such living together without its being oppressive and productive of destructive conflict: forgiveness is the discovery or the making of space for all to live together.*[12]

The search for peace and reconciliation through forgiveness takes into consideration the fact that if hurts, resentments, failures, bitterness, and humiliations go unchecked, there is a greater possibility of their being recycled.

There are times when "the price of peace is that justice – especially its retributive dimension – must be allowed to suffer political constraints."[13] Such situations are not ideal and can be frustrating for victims of atrocities. Yet, to make political and juridical compromises for the sake of making and keeping the peace is not altogether unethical. Social and political utility may be thought incompatible with certain forms of high-principled, philosophical ethics, but when it comes to framing ethics for the political life, utility cannot but be a factor in the ethical calculus.

The task of politicians and leaders to make and keep peace is also a moral responsibility. It is incumbent upon victims to demonstrate genuine forgiveness towards those who have not only wronged them, but are also likely to get away with it. Indeed, it may even be required of them to be "forgiving" of the less-than-ideal and imperfect justice that is inevitable for the sake of peace, and to be "reconciled" to their loss and suffering. This is itself a moral responsibility which victims have towards their political communities – especially if they recognise that the larger interest of their people is greater than their own personal interest, and that they have their own stakes in a more peaceful and secure future – one that may well be more protective of their own rights.

Forgiveness, Truth, and Reconciliation

It is often said that the first casualty in war is truth. This is especially true in cases of long-standing conflicts. One of the problems typically faced by reconciliation processes in conflict societies is that of "mytho-history," a selective and distorted memory whereby different groups of a conflict retrieve and recycle stories to create and cultivate a mythological past, exaggerating stories of atrocities and victimisation of the group by its enemies, while simultaneously downplaying, if not denying altogether, its own attitudes and acts of violence and injustice. Agreements on "bare facts" of past events are often hard to come by. This, in turn, means that there are often disagreements about what really happened. Each group in a conflict construes the conflict in a way that justifies its own violence but delegitimises that of the other side.

Yet the establishing of truth is a constitutive element of achieving reconciliation. Sometimes, "the whole truth" can be too overwhelming for individuals and groups to handle; victims are sometimes not keen to know "the truth" as it can re-open old wounds and thereby be detrimental to their healing process and the process of their reconciling with their loss. At other times, it may lead to revenge and further violence; indeed, sometimes truth-*telling* can be used as a destructive and disruptive weapon. From a Christian theological perspective, there is a sense in which concealment to a certain degree is necessary and appropriate. As Rowan Williams, former Archbishop of Canterbury, puts it:

> *Since the Fall concealment is necessary and good in the sense that there is plenty in human thought, feeling, and experience that* should not *be part of shared discourse. We are alienated, divided, and corrupted; but to bring this into speech (and to assume we thereby tell a better or fuller truth) is to collude with sin.*[14]

The point is not that the truth itself is unimportant, and much less that lies be told; it is rather that the *telling* of the truth is *sometimes* inappropriate. The question is also not whether or not truth is to be told, but, rather, *how, when, to whom,* and *why* it should be told.

If truth is sought for retributive purposes, it is unlikely that it will be willingly told by wrongdoers; if the truth is sought for reconciliatory purposes, it is more likely that truth-telling will be more forthcoming, as found, for example, in the South African Truth and Reconciliation Process.

From a Christian perspective, humans not only engage one another as fellow sinners but also as finite creatures. This means that they will not only be aware of their own wrongdoing against the other, but also of their own finite grasp of "the truth." In most cases of protracted conflict, there is a complex, often contradictory, set of narratives about "the truth" of the past.

To claim to have forgiven an enemy, while at the same time refusing to listen to their side of the story, of what happened, is to betray an unforgiving attitude. Alternatively, a willingness, even if begrudgingly, to listen to an enemy's version of events, however unpalatable, and contrary to one's version, reflects a charitable outlook and a respectful attitude – indeed, a forgiving spirit. It also reflects a genuine desire for reconciliation.

It is possible that through such exchanges, carried out in a spirit of docility, wrongdoers can come to acknowledge the truth of their guilt and begin to engage more fully in the process of reconciliation through the associated processes of repentance, confession, and restitution. Such a process can help victims to be more compassionate towards wrongdoers. To enter into debate with one's enemies over 'the truth' not only requires forgiveness, but can lead to further forgiveness, culminating in reconciliation.

Forgiveness, Justice, and Reconciliation

However, to gloss over injustices in the pursuit of reconciliation jeopardises not only justice but reconciliation itself. *The Kairos Document* from South Africa is the paradigmatic objection to reconciliation without justice:

> *In our situation in South Africa today it would be totally unchristian to plead for reconciliation and peace before the present injustices have been removed. Any such plea plays into the hands of the oppressor by trying to persuade those of us who are oppressed to accept our oppression and to become reconciled to the intolerable that are committed against us. That is not Christian reconciliation, it is sin. It is asking us to become accomplices in our own oppression, to become servants of the devil. No reconciliation is possible in South Africa* without justice.
>
> *What this means in practice is that no reconciliation, no forgiveness and no negotiations are possible* without repentance.[15]

While forgiveness is unilateral, unconditional, and free, reconciliation is a mutual and conditional process that requires some form of repentance, confession, and reparation. Without justice, as Martin Luther quipped, "If the lion lies with the lamb, the lamb must be replaced frequently." Reconciliation cannot take place unless justice is, even if imperfectly, enthroned. It also means that, while pursuits and expressions of justice remain legitimate and necessary, because they are situated in the context of forgiveness and love, not of revenge and resentment, genuine reconciliation – the fruit of grace and truth – becomes a real possibility.

Forgiveness and the Northern Ireland Conflict

Introduction

Many have undertaken studies of forgiveness in the politics of Northern Ireland. This chapter approaches the topic with one eye on the theory of forgiveness in politics already developed here and the other eye on forgiveness and politics in the Naga conflict.

The Northern Ireland Conflict: A Brief Sketch

The roots of the political conflict in Northern Ireland are usually traced to the early seventeenth century. This was when the British, after trying to conquer and colonise Ireland since the twelfth century, were able to establish an agricultural settlement, known as the plantation, in the area known as Ulster between 1610 and 1717. Following this, large numbers of Scottish Protestants came to Ulster and settled in lands confiscated from rebellious Irish natives. By the early eighteenth century, Scottish settlers outnumbered the Irish by five to three in Ulster. Understandably, the Catholic Irish natives resented being subjugated and displaced by the Protestant settlers, which resulted in the rise of Irish nationalism. This in turn, led to the rise of nationalism among the Protestant settlers, called the “unionists” or “loyalists,” who favoured the union of Ireland and Britain.

By the late nineteenth and early twentieth centuries, the conflict between the Protestant unionists and the Catholic republicans was deep and entrenched. In 1914, the Ulster Volunteer Force (UVF) was formed by the unionists to defeat the Irish nationalist movement through military force. It had more than one hundred thousand members and was armed with weapons smuggled from Germany. On the Irish side, the Irish Republican Army (IRA) formed with the goal of winning Irish independence through use of military force. The Easter of 1916 saw a violent uprising from the Irish. After heavy fighting, the Easter rebellion was crushed by the British government, its Irish leaders were executed, and martial law was imposed on Ireland. This only further inspired the Irish nationalistic cause and increased Irish resentment against the British.

By 1919, it became evident that the British were willing to withdraw from Ireland. This led to a bitter conflict between the Ulster Protestants, most of whom had come from Britain and favoured Ireland’s union with Britain, who opposed the withdrawal, and the Irish Catholics, who were opposed to British rule. As a compromise, the island of Ireland was partitioned in 1921, with the southern part becoming an independent state, while the northern part remained with the British as “Northern Ireland” or “Ulster.” However, the partition of Ireland, rather than resolving the issue, created a bitter divide in Northern Ireland, because there remained a substantial number of Irish Catholics who found themselves in the midst of a British Protestant majority and very unhappy with the partition settlement. At the same time, the Protestant unionists did not feel secure as they regarded the Catholic population in Northern Ireland as their enemy. There was also a great deal of economic disparity between the Protestants, who were the relatively prosperous ruling-class, and the Catholics, who were comparatively poorer and more deprived, a situation which was exacerbated by their being discriminated against in housing, employment, education, and political power and representation.

In the mid-1950s, the IRA adopted a policy to drive the British out of Northern Ireland. By the 1960s, the Catholic Irish in Northern Ireland began a non-violent civil rights movement to advance the cause of the Catholic Irish minority. This, in turn, was met with a response from the Protestant unionists, who feared that reforms undertaken by the Northern Irish government would go too far in favouring the Catholics. At this time, the Protestant Anti-Catholic rhetoric, led by the fundamentalist preacher, Rev Ian Paisley, fuelled the Protestant opposition to the proposed reforms in Northern Ireland and, in 1966, the Ulster Volunteer Force declared war on the IRA and started killing IRA militants. The UVF was outlawed by the Northern Irish government and the UVF went underground.

In 1968, what has come to be known as "the Troubles" began in Northern Ireland. In October of that year, there was a civil rights march in Londonderry, and while the organisers intended a non-violent protest, the protest soon turned violent when the Royal Ulster Constabulary (RUC) and a riot squad, both of which were predominantly comprised of Protestants, violently handled the protesters. The Northern Irish government announced some reforms, which was again rejected by the Protestants led by Ian

Paisley. In January 1969, the Catholic protesters organised another march from Belfast to Derry. The march was ambushed by a group of Protestants, who were assisted by the Ulster police. At this time, a more radical Irish nationalist group, the Provisional IRA (PIRA), which split from the "Official IRA," arose, and this group also came to be known as the "IRA."[16] The goals of the PIRA was to eject Britain from Northern Ireland, the unification of Ireland, and the establishment of a socialist republic in Ireland. In 1972, the official IRA signed a cease-fire agreement with the British government, while the PIRA continued with their violent modus operandi, which included bombings, assassinations, kidnappings, extortion, robberies, and punishment beatings.

As the violence continued, the authority and legitimacy of the Northern Irish government was challenged by both sides of the conflict. Then, in 1969, British troops were sent to Ireland. As the British military forces countered the violence of the IRA, they soon came to be seen as the enemy of the Catholic Irish. The imposition of a curfew, intensive door-to-door searches in Catholic communities, imprisonment of violent Catholics activists without trial, the use of brutality in interrogation, all led to increased resentment among the Irish Catholics against the British, and resulted in further violent activities on the part of the nationalists. On 30th January 1972, the British military forces opened fire on a protest march in Londonderry, killing thirteen people. This event came to be known as Bloody Sunday. In all these events, the civilian population became caught up under both British Army brutality and the continued IRA violent campaigns.

Up until the end of the "Troubles" in the 1990s, it is estimated that approximately three and a half thousand people were killed and forty thousand people were seriously injured. In 1984, there was an attack at the Conservative party conference on the British mainland by the IRA, in which five people were killed, and the Prime Minister, Margaret Thatcher narrowly escaped. The British Prime Minister's residence, 10 Downing Street, London, was also attacked in 1991 when the Prime Minister, John Major, was at home.

In 1976, the British government announced that persons convicted of crimes related to the Troubles would be treated as ordinary criminals and not with the special category status of "political prisoners." This change of status for the nationalist prisoners resulted in protests among the nationalist prisoners; ten prisoners died due to their consequent hunger strikes in 1981. The British government eventually made concessions and the hunger strikes ended.

In 1985, there was an agreement known as the Hillsborough Agreement, which emphasised the need for reform in the North, the need for a majority approval of change in the status of Northern Ireland, and acknowledged the necessity of input from the Republic of Ireland. However, the Agreement provoked angry protests from the Unionists, who began to riot and attack British military forces.

While the violence continued, positive developments were also occurring. There was increasing cooperation between the governments of Britain and the Republic of Ireland. Sinn Fein, the political wing of the IRA, also began taking and emphasising an increasingly political approach. Although hard line nationalist groups continued to take a military approach for the removal of the British from Ireland, they were increasingly alienated from the Catholic people by their violence. In August 1994, the IRA declared a cease-fire, citing conflict-fatigue and their fear of alienating the population.

The unionist paramilitary groups also announced a cease-fire in September, announcing that they were terminating their military operations.

On 10th April 1998, an agreement, known as the Good Friday Agreement was reached. Among other things, the Good Friday Agreement gave space for the resolution of differences by political means and not violence, noting the Northern Irish right to self-determination, and set out that both the United Kingdom and the Republic of Ireland would recognise the will of the people of Ireland in their future political affiliation. The Agreement also stated a commitment to human rights, freedom of political thought and religion, and the right of all persons to equal opportunity in all social and economic activity, regardless of class, creed, disability, gender, or ethnicity. It also stated its commitment to reconciliation, and the decommissioning of arms of all paramilitary groups, both on the nationalist and the unionist sides. Although a number of violent events have since threatened the Agreement, the Agreement has held out.

Understanding the Northern Ireland Conflict

The conflict in Northern Ireland has long defied resolution. That is in large part because it has defied explanation, and that is in spite of the fact that, in proportion to size, Northern Ireland is probably the most heavily researched area on earth. According to Senator George Mitchell, an American who played a vital role in negotiating the Good Friday Agreement, "The conflict in Northern Ireland is a meta-conflict. That is to say that there is conflict over what the conflict is about,"[17] with actors and analysts giving different explanations.

Some argue that at the heart of the Irish problems is the unwanted presence of the British in Ireland. As Gerry Adams, a key leader of Sinn Féin, put it, "By its very nature the British presence is not and never has been a just or peaceful presence and, because of this, relationships between British and Irish people have been poisoned. When the root cause of violence in Ireland is removed then and only then will the violence cease."[18]

Some argue that religion is at the heart of the problem, with either Catholicism or Protestantism being the root cause of the problem. The second explanation argues that it is a clash of cultures that is at the heart of the Northern Irish problem.

Yet another argument gives weight to economic inequality or economic opportunism as being at the heart of the conflict, implying that the pursuit of personal profit has been a more important motive than ideology in explaining violence.

It is obvious even to an outside observer that there is no single, explanation for the conflict, and according to Mitchell, single accounts cannot get to the heart of divisions in Northern Ireland, "as they all simplify, and exaggerate their preferred explanation." So how then do the different forces and factors relate to one another?

One of the most helpful – and, to my mind, correct – analytical approaches to the conflict is given by Ruane and Todd in their book *Dynamics of Conflict in Northern Ireland.*[19] According to them, the conflict in Northern Ireland is best approached within a "system of relationships" that has three interlocking levels of division, difference and dominance. They argue that, over the centuries, Ireland underwent a slow and complex process of an island-wide communal division, which was completed only in the late nineteenth century.

This was followed by partition, which created new conditions for community formation and division, without displacing those of the pre-partition period.

In addition to communal division lies the difference of religion (Catholicism versus various strands of Protestantism), ethnicity (Gaelic-Irish, Old English, New English, Scottish) and colonialism (native versus settler). These dimensions of difference have intertwined and conflicted with each other since the sixteenth and seventeenth centuries. These dimensions of difference also overlapped: the Protestants were predominantly of English or Scottish stock, came in as settlers, were imbued with a self-perception of civility and superiority, and were later overwhelmingly unionist; the Catholics, on the other hand, were predominantly of Gaelic-Irish stock, with a perception of displaced natives, regarded as backward, and later became overwhelmingly nationalists.

Furthermore, Britain needed the loyal Protestants to retain Ireland for the Crown; the Protestants needed Britain to maintain their position. The result was that the Protestants were accorded power in Ireland. This alienated the Irish Catholics and threatened the established order. The only way of changing the situation was by allowing the Irish equal participation in political power. The problem with such a move was that it faced Protestant resistance without guaranteeing Irish loyalty. This dynamic of dominance, dependence and inequality continued after the formation of Northern Ireland and exists to this day.

Forgiveness in Northern Ireland

In studying Northern Ireland from the perspective of forgiveness, it is very easy to look for the absence of forgiveness rather than its presence. Yet, Northern Ireland is home to many of the most powerful stories of forgiveness in the context of political violence.

The most well-known is that offered by Gordon Wilson, whose daughter, Marie, was among the eleven people killed by an IRA bomb during a ceremony at the Enniskillen War Memorial in 1987 in honour of Britain's war dead. Wilson's act of forgiveness was echoed in the world media and in Queen Elizabeth II's Christmas Day address that year. On the other side of the sectarian divide is the story of Michael McGoldrick's unilateral forgiveness of those Protestant paramilitaries who shot dead his son, Michael, on 8th July 1996. Another story of personal forgiveness by a direct victim is the story of Karen McKeown, a totally innocent twenty-year-old, who , was shot in the neck from point-blank range by a gunman as she left an evening service in her church in East Belfast. This was in retaliation for another attack in the area the previous day. Karen, totally paralysed but mentally alert, lived for three weeks in the intensive care unit before she died on 16th October 1982. The forgiveness that the remarkable young woman displayed was truly transcending. Kerr, recounting her story, says, "Shortly before she died, Karen said to her mother, 'Mum, think of the mother of the man who shot me. How must she feel? I'm sorry he did it, but I am more sorry for him.'"[20] These stories are powerful and moving.

Such personal acts of forgiveness can contribute to the emotional healing of the victims and create deep impressions of people on the possibilities of human forgiveness. These stories also serve as prophetic acts that point to a higher reality, and serve as reminders that violence can be transcended. In certain exceptional cases, such personal forgiveness can result in remarkable stories of repentance of perpetrators and reconciliation between victims and perpetrators. One such story is that of Florence Cobb, whose husband, an RUC inspector, was murdered by a member of the Ulster Defence Association (UDA). Mrs Cobb wrote a letter of forgiveness to her husband's killer who was in prison. The killer, in turn, showed it to another fellow member and prisoner, who was so moved that he invited Mrs. Cobb to the Maze prison. The prisoner met with Mrs Cobb and they fell in love. Some of these personal acts of forgiveness have resulted in larger movements that aimed intentionally at having greater social impact. The founding of the Cross Group by Maura Kiely, who lost her nineteen-year-old son to loyalist gunmen is one such example. Other examples include the work of Máiread Corrigan-Maguire and Betty Williams of Women for Peace, and the work of Una O'Higgins O'Malley, founder of the Centre for Reconciliation at Glencree.

However, these acts have little political effect in terms of mitigating long-standing antagonism and breaking broad-based cycles of violence driven by strong political ideologies and purpose. Only rarely can an individual by themselves stem the rushing tide of violence.

Beyond the personal level, there have been more *public* words and gestures of political forgiveness and repentance coming from high-profile leaders and groups. Perhaps the most notable and publicised gesture of public repentance from a clergyman came from the Archbishop of Canterbury, George Carey. In a sermon in Christ

Church Cathedral, Dublin, on 18th March 1994, Carey said, "As an English Churchman, I am aware of just how much we English need to ask forgiveness for our often brutal domination and crass insensitivity in the eight hundred years of history of our relationships with Ireland."[21] These words of repentance were reciprocated by the Cardinal Cahal B. Daly on 22nd January 1995, when he said:

> *On this occasion of the visit of an Irish Roman Catholic Primate to Canterbury Cathedral, I wish to ask forgiveness from the people of this land for the wrongs and hurts inflicted by Irish people upon the people of this country on many occasions during our shared history, and particularly in the past 25 years. I believe that this reciprocal recognition of the need to forgive and to be forgiven is a necessary condition for proper Christian and human and indeed political relationships between our two islands in the future.*[22]

Such words by church leaders, although not without controversy, are hardly surprising, given that forgiveness is commonly thought to be most "at home" in the church. However, when these words come from politicians, they can be much more significant and controversial. Such an act came in June 1997 from Prime Minister Tony Blair when he made an unprecedented statement regarding the 1840s Irish famine:

> *That one million people should have died in what was then part of the richest and most powerful nation in the world is something that still causes pain as we reflect on it today. Those who governed in London at the time failed their*

> *people through standing by while a crop failure turned into a massive human tragedy.*[23]

Whether or not what Blair said can be interpreted strictly as "repentance" is a matter of debate. His words were, nevertheless, graciously received by his Irish counterpart, Prime Minister John Bruton, who noted that it would provide a better basis for working together in the future.

Besides these high-profile priests and politicians, paramilitary groups have also been involved in public political apologies. The most significant public words of apology from a paramilitary group came in July 2002, during the thirtieth anniversary of Bloody Friday, when the IRA issued a statement of apology in the republican newspaper *An Phoblacht* (Republican News).

These political apologies and forgiveness by high-profile representatives and groups have, no doubt, been significant and valuable. Their value is, however, at best, limited. And words, unless they go beyond verbal formulae, run the danger of being trivialised.

Merely looking out for explicit use of the term "forgiveness" is not the most helpful or promising way for studying forgiveness in politics. A more helpful, if unusual and difficult, approach is to explore actual political events, and ask whether or not on an underlying, even if invisible, forgiveness might be discerned in them. In what follows, one of the most historic events in Northern Irish politics will be mined for such an exploration.

Forgiveness and the Good Friday Agreement

It is believed by a large population of the world that there was forgiveness on Good Friday, 33 AD. The question is: Was there forgiveness on Good Friday, 1998 AD, with the Good Friday Agreement which was by all accounts a historic agreement? The document provides the basis of the new Northern Ireland that has since moved, if ever so imperfectly, from a seemingly intractable conflict to an increasingly hopeful peace. The parties to the Agreement commended it to the people for their endorsement through the "Declaration of Support" (see Appendix 1).

Most writers on the Northern Irish conflict do not care to look for forgiveness in the Good Friday Agreement; they assume *a priori* that it is not there. Others who care to look for it, do not find it, and call the achievement of the Good Friday Agreement "Peace without Forgiveness or Reconciliation."[24] Whether or not the achievement of Good Friday Agreement was "forgiveness" depends, of course, on what one means by forgiveness and the criteria one sets for it.

I consider the Good Friday Agreement as offering a good, if imperfect, case of political forgiveness, even if it may not fit snugly into a neatly ordered theoretical framework of forgiveness. In the first place, the matrix of events known as the Northern Ireland "peace process," of which the Good Friday Agreement is the most significant part, could never have happened without a good measure of operative forgiveness by the parties involved.

It was not, however, just the religious peacemakers, but the conflicting individuals and parties who had to operate with forgiveness. Take, for instance, the then leader of the Social

Democratic and Labour Party (SDLP), John Hume, and his direct secret talks with both the British government and Sinn Féin. Heavily criticised from all sides in the political spectrum especially for his continued talks with the enemies, Hume had to defend himself saying, "I'm a politician, politics is the alternative to war, politics is about dialogue, I'm about dialogue. I'll talk to anyone about it, that doesn't mean I approve of what they stand for."[25] Despite the heavy criticism and frequent setbacks, it is widely agreed that Hume's talks provided a significant background to the process that led first to the 1985 Anglo-Irish Agreement, and later the Good Friday Agreement. Despite the personal strain in straddling those different groups, Hume decided that the bad acts of his enemies did not define them, he did not look for revenge, but a new relationship with them. These are precisely some of the elements that make up forgiveness.

In 1998, Hume won the Nobel Peace Prize for his efforts. But what is true in his case is also true for many of the others who were involved in the peace process. It was a difficult moment of adjustment for people on many parts of the spectrum. Quite a few of those at the table could recall the names of friends, colleagues and relatives killed in the Troubles; they could also glance round the room and see people whom they held responsible for deaths.

It was against such a background of deep animosity and hatred that the painfully slow and precarious politics of forgiveness took place. Those at the table could have walked away from the table as some individuals did; they could have stayed away from the table as some parties did. But the fact that they were willing, even if begrudgingly, to do politics instead of war, "to get on with those who tried to murder," meant that each individual participant and party had to operate with a good measure of forgiveness.

Jonathan Powell, Prime Minister Blair's Chief of Staff during the time of the peace process, has also given a first-hand, insider account of how the precariously fragile process took place in his book, *Great Hatred, Little Room.* He says, "One of the lessons that comes most starkly out of the Northern Ireland experience is the importance of maintaining contact. It is very difficult for governments in democracies to be seen to be talking to terrorists who are killing their people unjustifiably. But it is precisely your enemies, rather than your friends, you should talk to if you want to resolve a conflict."[26] To talk to one's enemies, to maintain contact with them, is an essentially political activity, which requires forgiveness.

It could, of course, be objected that the label "forgiveness" is inappropriate for what transpired, for this kind of forgiveness – if at all – is very impure or imperfect, and the individuals and parties involved, would not necessarily call their actions and attitudes "forgiveness". Other terms such as accommodation, tolerance, mutual respect, forbearance, or compromise, negotiation could more accurately describe the actions and attitudes. Forgiveness involves more than any or all of these. However, there is seldom, if ever, "pure" and "perfect" forgiveness in human relationships. Imperfect forgiveness is often all that humans can hope to achieve in their finitude and sinful predicament. Even if the forgiveness of the peace process was impure, it is perhaps the most that one could expect, and it is, I suggest, good enough.

Forgiveness always involves forbearance and a willingness to negotiate, and they are necessary conditions. It could be argued that the forgiveness in operation during the peace process leading to the Good Friday Agreement contains *all* the elements that constitute what is the most widely-used and accepted definition of political forgiveness, that it is an act that joins moral truth, forbearance, empathy, and commitment to repair a fractured human relation. The parties held on to what was their own respective moral and historical truths, employed a great deal of forbearance from revenge, had empathy for the opposing parties' perspectives, and displayed their willingness to repair their fractured human relations.

In his essay, "Forgiving Enemies in Ireland,"[27] Biggar argues that whatever reconciliation that Northern Ireland comes to enjoy in the near future will inevitably be a "reconciliation of partisans." By that he means that the shared future of Northern Ireland will comprise and be built by people who hold to different views and judgements about Northern Ireland, not least its past. "Peace will have to be made by and between enemies," he goes on to say, "Reconciliation will have to happen between those who continue to disagree about what caused the Troubles and about who is basically to blame for them." If there can be reconciliation among partisans in Northern Ireland, there can also be, I claim, forgiveness among them.

The Good Friday Agreement and Justice

But what does the Good Friday Agreement make of the question of justice? The Good Friday Agreement was controversial because, for many, justice was sacrificed at the altar of peace. Although this appears to be the case, the Good Friday Agreement denies neither primary justice nor retributive justice. There is an affirmation of primary justice in the Agreement when it declares, "We are committed to partnership, equality and mutual respect as the basis of relationships within Northern Ireland, between North and South, and between these islands." The Agreement states that it recognises the will of the Northern Irish people as to their future political identity and affiliation. It also states a commitment to human rights – including the right to freedom and expression of religion; the right to pursue democratically national and political aspirations; the right to seek constitutional change by peaceful and legitimate means; the right to freely choose one's place of residence; the right to equal opportunity in all social and economic activity, regardless of class, creed, disability, gender or ethnicity; the right to freedom from sectarian harassment; and the right of women to full and equal political participation. It importantly acknowledges the suffering of the victims and makes provision for support and reparation. In a society like Northern Ireland where there has long been a violation and denial of primary justice, such a commitment to equality at all these fundamental levels and dimensions of relationship is surely a step in the right direction as far as the question of primary justice is concerned.

This question of primary justice is, however, not nearly as controversial as that of retributive justice. Although the Agreement recognises the suffering of victims and sets up institutions for their support and reparation, one of the most controversial elements of the Good Friday Agreement is the provision for the early release of paramilitary prisoners, the vast majority of whom were released by the year 2000. This turned out to be extremely controversial because many saw it as a compromise on the question of retributive justice.

However, in an article, "Peace and Justice: A Limited Reconciliation",[28] Biggar says that the tension between peace and justice arising out of the Good Friday Agreement is so only within a particular understanding of criminal justice as strict retributive punishment of wrongdoers. He goes on to argue that this tension can be significantly relaxed once the usual understanding of justice as retributive punishment of perpetrators is revised. For Biggar, "justice is not *primarily* about the punishment of the perpetrator but about the vindication of victims, both direct and indirect." The basic form that vindication of victims takes is that of recognising their injury, and thereby acknowledging their dignity. This form of criminal justice in which vindication of the victim is primary, and the punishment of the perpetrator is secondary and subordinate to it, Biggar claims, is also biblical. In saying all this, Biggar does not mean to deny the place of punishment in justice. For him, punishment is properly retributive insofar as it is a response to one who has committed a crime; insofar as it annuls the unfair advantage that a criminal gains through crime; insofar as it expresses the proper opprobrium of the community towards the crime; and insofar as there is some conventional or symbolic proportion between it and the penalty.

Biggar's point is that the Good Friday Agreement was not a sacrifice of justice at the altar of peace, to which I would add it was also not, thereby, a sacrifice of justice at the altar of forgiveness.

Since 2002, when Biggar was writing, much more progress has been made in the Northern Ireland peace process, albeit interspersed with occasional significant setbacks and bouts of violence. Biggar's prediction that most of the paramilitary forces would not return to violence has been proven, on the whole, correct. In September 2005, it was announced that the IRA had put all its weapons "beyond use." In June 2009, the Ulster Volunteer Force & Red Hand Commando UVF/RHC announced that it had put its weapons "totally, and irreversibly, beyond use." In another statement on the same day, the Ulster Defence Association (UDA) also announced that they had started the process of decommissioning.

The Good Friday Agreement can be interpreted as a form of forgiveness in Northern Irish politics. As a multi-party agreement, it resulted from a bringing together and reconciliation of enemies, serving as a way to a better and more hopeful future that Northern Ireland has come to enjoy since the Agreement. This is a future neither disjointed from the past nor determined by it, all of which involved a good measure of forgiveness.

The Naga Story

Introduction

Having looked at forgiveness in politics and the Northern Ireland conflict, I now turn to the Naga conflict.

During the last six decades or more, the Nagas have been embroiled in one of the world's longest but least-known violent nationalist conflicts and it has claimed thousands of lives.

The Naga conflict originally began as a struggle for Naga independence, and initially displayed remarkable Naga solidarity founded upon romantic idealism. It has, however, long since degenerated into a cycle of factional feuds that has caught Naga society in a vortex of hatred, violence, and vengeance.[29]

The Nagas

The Nagas are a people group consisting of several tribes who occupy a contiguous tract of mountainous territory between India and Myanmar. In India, they are found in the north-eastern Indian states of Nagaland, Manipur, Assam, and Arunachal Pradesh; in Myanmar, they are found in Sagaing Division and Kachin state. It is estimated that the Naga population is between 3.5 and 4 million people with 2 million living within the state of Nagaland itself.

Before the turn of the twentieth century, there was no "Naga identity" as such. People did not identify as a collective beyond their particular village or tribe. Each village was a sovereign republic and their small world was one of internecine headhunting feuds among themselves and with their neighbours in the plains, although every now and again they came together in the face of a common enemy.

About 90 per cent of Nagas are Baptist Christians. Christianity first came to the Nagas through the American Baptist missionaries in the second half of the nineteenth century but the massive conversions took place only after the independence movement gained momentum. The predominance of Christianity in Nagaland has important political implications – both negative and positive.

The Nagas against the British

While many trace the beginnings of the Naga conflict to the early part of the twentieth century, Nagas claim that the roots of the conflict can be found much earlier in the Treaty of Yandabo of 1826. This Anglo-Burmese treaty severed Naga country and the Naga people, some claim without their knowledge, with one-half falling under Burmese administration and the other half on the Indian side. Following this event, the British made a number of expeditions against the Nagas which were fiercely resisted. In 1866-67, the British set up a headquarters in Naga territory as their "first permanent footing." In 1879-1880, after a bloody battle, the last organised Naga resistance to the British fell, and the Nagas officially came under the British administration. The British thus made the Naga Hills a British district in 1881. There were, however, many Naga areas in the east that were not administered by the British. The British called these the "un-administered areas".

"Naga national consciousness" was awakened when some twenty Nagas came together and formed the Naga Club in 1918. In the late 1920s, as the possibility of the British leaving India arose, the Nagas also began considering the possibility of independence. In 1929, when the Indian Statutory Commission visited the Naga Hills, the Naga Club presented a memorandum to the Commission, which came to be known as the 1929 Simon Commission Memorandum. The Memorandum stated that before the British conquered Naga country, the Nagas had never been conquered. While it conceded that "We have no unity among us and it is really the British Government that is holding us together now," it also pleaded, "If the British Government, however, wants to throw us away, it should not be left to the mercy of the people who could never subjugate us, but leave us alone to determine our future as in the ancient times."

The Government of India Act in 1935 was the outcome of the Commission's report, and put the Naga Hills under what the Act called "Excluded Areas" that were left directly under the British Crown's Representative. Nagas interpreted this as of great significance, taking it to imply a kind of special provision or arrangement that excluded the Naga Hills from the rest of India. However, such an interpretation was unwarranted.

In April 1945, with the imminent departure of the British from India, the Naga Hills District Tribal Council was formed, comprising representative tribal councils from various tribes. This Council replaced the earlier Naga Club. In 1946, this Council became the Naga National Council (NNC), which became the umbrella political organisation for the struggle for Naga independence.

From 26th to 28th June 1947, discussions were held between the Government of India and representatives of the Naga National Council, leading to the Nine Point, or Hydari Agreement, which granted far-reaching autonomy to the NNC. However, the ninth point proved problematic. It stated:

> *The Governor of Assam, as the Agent of the Government of the Indian Union, will have a special responsibility for a period of 10 years to ensure the observance of the agreement, at the end of this period the Naga Council will be asked whether they require the above agreement to be extended for a further period or a new agreement regarding the future of Naga people arrived at.*

The Nagas interpreted this clause as granting them the right to self-determination, including the right to be independent, at the end of the ten-year period. The Indian side denied this, and the Constituent Assembly of India refused to ratify it. In July 1947, a Naga delegation met with Mahatma Gandhi, where Gandhi is reported to have said: "We do not want the British and they are going. If you say that you are not Indians and your country does not belong to India, then the matter ends there. Nobody will force you to join the Indian Union."

There was, however, no significant progress in the understanding between the incoming Indian government and the NNC. Thus, on 14th August 1947, a day before the Indian declaration of independence, the NNC declared independence. India ignored this declaration. In 1950, A. Z. Phizo, also known as "the father of Naga nationalism," was elected NNC President, and the Naga independence movement gained momentum with the launching of a campaign of civil non-cooperation with India. On 16th May 1951, a plebiscite conducted by the NNC claimed that 99 per cent of Nagas supported independence. The next year, Nagas boycotted the first Indian general election. The Government of India responded by banning the NNC and issuing arrest warrants against its leaders, who then went underground. In March 1953, the Indian Prime Minister, Nehru, and his Burmese counterpart, U Nu, came to Kohima, today the capital town of Nagaland. This event, however, took an unfortunate turn when the Nagas leaders were refused – perhaps without Nehru's own knowledge – a meeting with the Prime Minister. This led to 4000 people walking out from the public meeting that had been arranged. Thus, by the time the Prime Minister arrived and ascended the rostrum along with U Nu, the entire Naga audience was absent excepting a few government servants left at the place of the meeting. It is tragic that this significant visit turned into a debacle. A settlement of the Naga problem would have to involve the Governments of India and Burma, and here were both the leaders of the two nations in person. Nehru and U Nu could have settled the Naga problem between them without too much difficulty, but it is said that Nehru never forgot the insult.

In September 1954, Phizo declared the formation of the People's Sovereign Republic of Free Nagaland. Soon after that, the movement took a violent turn. The Indian army moved into the Naga areas and the Indo-Naga war began in 1955. In 1956, the NNC formed the Naga Central Government – renamed the Federal Government of Nagaland (FGN) in 1959 – and its own "army." From what initially began as opportunistic guerrilla warfare between the world's largest standing army and a band of rag-tag guerrillas, the conflict soon flared up and caught the whole Naga civilian population up in its wake.

During this time, there was nearly one security troop member for every adult male Naga in the Naga areas. The Indian armed forces were armed and protected with legislation enacted and promulgated by the Indian Parliament. These Acts effectively gave the Indian armed forces unrestricted power to carry out their military operations in the Naga areas without any political or legal interference. The Armed Forces (Special Powers) Act, which remains in force to this day, not only grants sweeping powers to the armed forces to destroy property, search premises, and make arrests without warrant, but also empowers a non-commissioned army officer to "fire upon or otherwise use force, even to the causing of death," any person on mere suspicion. The Act also guarantees that legal action cannot be taken against members of the Indian armed forces for anything done, or purported to be done, under the Act, without the sanction of the Government of India. Protected by such legislation, human rights violations became rampant and routine. Between 1955 and 1956, the Indian security forces burned down more than 645 out of some 860 Naga villages. Thousands of deaths occurred from shooting, torture, starvation, amongst other brutalities.

The Nagas against Themselves

When the violent conflict with India began, rifts amid the Nagas, including within the Naga National Conference began to emerge. On the one side were the extremist group while on the other side were the moderate group who had advocated a non-violent approach. The more militant group began threatening and killing the moderates who disagreed with the confrontational stance that they were adopting and also those Nagas who were serving under the Government of India. During this time, a prominent Naga leader and architect of Naga nationalism, T. Sakhrie, who advocated for a non-violent, political approach, was also brutally killed by the hard-line nationalists.

In 1958, representatives of the Naga People's Convention (NPC) entered into negotiations with the Government of India regarding the potential formation of a state within the Indian Union. Although there were a number of prominent NPC leaders who objected to this move, nevertheless on 1st December 1963, the state of Nagaland was declared as the sixteenth state within the Indian Union. The NNC refused to recognise statehood as they considered it a significant setback to independence. Thus, rather than quell the nationalist movement, it intensified intra-Naga political rivalries and complicated the Naga political landscape.

A significant step towards peace in Nagaland was made in 1964. By this time, "The Nagas' desire for Peace was as deep, if not deeper, than their desire for freedom."[30] Through the endeavours of the Nagaland Baptist Church Council (NBCC) and its Peace Mission, representatives of the Federal Government of Nagaland and the

Government of India signed an armistice treaty, The Cease Fire Agreement in August 1964. The Agreement, which came into effect at midnight 6th September 1964, was also meant to lead to peace talks between the governments. Thanksgiving services were held in every town and village in Nagaland. To this day, 6th September is commemorated as Nagaland Peace Day.

A number of things, however, led to the collapse of the Agreement in 1972. First of all, there were allegations and counter-allegations of violations of the Agreement's terms between the two governments. Second, internal political wrangles, rifts, and betrayals led to a split within the Naga government along tribal lines. This, together with a number of killings and attempted assassinations on both sides, led the Indian Government to unilaterally withdraw from the Agreement in 1972. Hostilities resumed, and Nagaland was once again plunged into another episode of violence.

A major political development took place in 1975 when, on 11th November, the Shillong Accord was signed between the Governor, representing the Government of India, and certain "representatives of the underground organisations." Although the Accord was signed under the terrible pressure of Indian army brutality and Naga public attrition, it included the unconditional acceptance of the Constitution of India. The agreement confused the Naga public and fractured the Naga movement. While the official NNC distanced itself from the Accord, some leading underground members condemned it as a treacherous sell-out. These nationalists broke away from the NNC because Phizo, who had by then fled to and settled in London but remained NNC President, was silent on the issue despite several pleas from them to denounce it. Thus 1980 saw the formation of the

National Socialist Council of Nagaland (NSCN). Since then, "The Accordists, as they came to be called, were hounded by those who opposed it and several were killed."[31] The gulf between the so-called "Accordists" and the "Non-accordists" remains as wide as ever, and has claimed the lives of many.

In 1990, Phizo's death in London led to further divisions within the original NNC. Currently, in addition to the Nagaland state government that functions under the purview of the Indian constitution, there are at least five major nationalist groups, divided along ideological and (partly) tribal lines, each running its own parallel government.

In 1997, a number of ceasefires were agreed with India, and while they have drastically decreased the conflict level between nationalists and the Indian armed forces, they have resulted in institutionalised extortion, kidnappings and targeted killings that have all become part of everyday life in Nagaland.

Anatomy of Deeply Divided Societies

In his book, *Building Peace: Sustainable Reconciliation in Divided Societies*,[32] John Lederach, an American Professor of International Peacebuilding at the University of Notre Dame, Indiana, delineates what he calls "characteristics of deeply divided societies," referring to societies that are experiencing "armed conflicts." He outlines a number of starting points which can be illustrated by the Naga situation, describing it as a conflict taking place in the developing world, located within the boundaries of a defined state (namely, India and/or Burma); many of the conflictants operate out of neighbouring regions (such as Burma, Bangladesh, and Nepal), weaponry and other assistance flow in from neighbouring and more distant nations (such as China and Pakistan), and that the conflict has been a major contributor to the instability of the region.

He then identifies four interacting factors of such deeply divided societies. Identity tends to form along narrow lines other than those of national citizenship; there is autonomy of action within groups and subgroups, meaning that power is diffuse and the command of individual leaders over their respective groups is never easy to assess, making representation and decision-making for the population difficult.

Furthermore, the conflicts that these societies find themselves caught in are often protracted with the perceptions and fear, and hatred between groups are deep-rooted, passing from one generation to another. Over time, conflict comes to be accepted by all parties involved as the way of group survival and self-preservation, and not as something that is oppressive and detrimental to all involved.

The fourth characteristic of most intra-national contemporary conflicts is the absence or limited availability of formal governmental or international mechanisms for dealing with the conflict. The founding charters of international organisations, such as the United Nations Organisation (UNO), lay out strict limitations against intervention in the internal affairs of its member-states. Moreover, the traditional paradigms of these organisations in approaching conflicts remain limited to international, statist diplomacy. Thus, given that most of these conflicts are internal or intra-national by nature, recourse to resolving conflicts through international bodies becomes very limited.

These four characteristics of deeply divided societies articulate the predicament of contemporary Naga society, with an ever-narrowing of identities. The Naga conflict began with the idealistic assertion of a "Naga identity" that was opposed to Indian national citizenship. As the conflict progressed, there has been an ever-increasing tendency towards a return to smaller groups, increasingly along narrow tribal affiliations. The consequence of this is a confused diffusion of power and the absence of an effective centralised authority. The Naga conflict is also one of the longest-standing conflicts in the world, and most Nagas living today have little sense of life without conflict.

Forgiveness and Reconciliation in Nagaland: Starts, False-starts, Non-starters, and Fresh-starts

Despite the fact that Naga society remains a deeply divided and violent society, there have also been many stories of forgiveness and reconciliation by prominent individuals and families. Both the former Chief Minister of Nagaland, S. C. Jamir, and the current Chief Minister, Neiphiu Rio, have publicly declared their forgiveness on the National Socialist Council of Nagaland/Nagalim-Isak-Muivah who tried to assassinate them on different occasions. The story of how the Kevichusa family-clan declared forgiveness after the killing of two prominent members of the family is also well-known locally. There are many individuals, families, and communities, who have, in the aftermath of terrible atrocities, quietly, away from the glare of publicity, moved on with their lives, forgivingly.

A major effort towards "Naga reconciliation" took place at a public event called the "Naga National Reconciliation Function" on 20th December 2001 in Kohima. Jointly organised by the Naga Hoho, an apex Naga tribal body, and the Nagaland Christian Forum (NCF), the event was attended by tribal representatives of about 35 Naga tribes. The event was well-attended and emotionally charged. During that occasion, leaders of the various Naga tribes took a solemn oath pledging that Nagas are one family and will work towards the Nagas growing as a people, examining the ways in which others have been hurt so that forgiving and being forgiven will become possible.

From 2002 to 2006, other attempts at healing and reconciliation have been made with some success. In February 2008, a full-time Christian prayer group known as *Shisha Hoho* called for a three-day Naga peace convention at Dimapur, the main commercial city of Nagaland. Although poorly attended, during the convention, the idea of forming a Naga forum for peace was floated and The Forum for Naga Reconciliation was born on 25th March 2008. This has come to be the most effective movement for reconciliation. It is to an assessment of the Forum for Naga Reconciliation that this book will now turn.

The Forum for Naga Reconciliation: An Assessment

Introduction

Since the formation of the Forum for Naga Reconciliation, it is widely acknowledged that it has had considerable success in reducing violence, bringing together the various nationalist factions together for political negotiations and fostering a genuine sense of hope for Naga reconciliation.

One of the major outcomes of these engagements was the so-called "Covenant of Reconciliation," jointly signed on 13th June 2009 by the leaders of three major factions, resolving "to continue to work together in a spirit of love, non-violence, peace and respect to resolve outstanding issues amongst us".

In September 2009, again under the aegis of the Forum for Naga Reconciliation, the three major factions, made a declaration pledging 'to cease all forms of offensive activities *in toto*." The ceasefire among the groups has, on the whole, held out. On 29th February 2012, a major public gathering, attended by about 50,000 people, passed a number of resolutions supporting the on-going reconciliation process.

After sixty years of conflict, the Nagas are suffering from attrition and conflict fatigue. The Forum for Naga Reconciliation has sought to be broad-based and is comprised of representatives from various frontal organisations, including church leaders. Resolute in its work, a reconciliation project "A Journey of Common Hope," has now completed four years of sustained effort and engagement.

Sustained support and sponsorship of international groups, such as the American Baptists and the English Quakers, has proved invaluable for the reconciliation process. There have also been public letters of support for Forum for Naga Reconciliation from Nobel Peace laureates such as President Jimmy Carter and Archbishop Desmond Tutu. The leadership and personality of Rev Dr Wati Aier, the Convenor of the Forum for Naga Reconciliation, is another important factor in its success. The Baptist World Alliance (BWA) not only passed an official resolution supporting the work of the Forum for Naga Reconciliation, but gave Dr Wati Aier, its prestigious BWA Denton and Janice Lotz Human Rights Award in 2011.

Dr Wati displays a remarkable determination not to condemn anyone, but seeks to engage with all while not condoning their violence, trying to find a way to end the killing, and defining his Christian role as the interpreter of each to all. He is not associated with any specific groups and two doctorates from the United States give him intellectual and academic credentials added to which are strong religious credentials. Using unconventional methods in the reconciliation process, the Forum for Naga Reconciliation has organised 12 so-called "special programmes" including football matches, special church services, joint social work, and joint food and relief distribution. The first football match in Chiang Mai "loosened" the participants involved in the talks: "From the day after the football match, you could see that the whole atmosphere of the political talks was in a positive direction. The football matches also helped in drawing the public into the reconciliation process."

If it has been unconventional in its practices, Forum for Naga Reconciliation has also been unabashed in its Christian basis and rhetoric with Christian devotions, hymns, and prayers The Forum for Naga Reconciliation's basis for Naga reconciliation has, however, not just been religious; it has also been resolutely political. Again and again, it emphasises the point that the basis of Naga reconciliation is "the historical and political rights of the Nagas." At first glance, this basis of reconciliation appears curious, yet all the Naga nationalist groups claim to be fighting for the Naga right to independence. This basis serves as a guarantee that the Naga nationalist struggle will not be sacrificed at the altar of reconciliation. It gives enough space for different interpretations as to what the historical and political rights of Nagas might actually be – from full independence from India, to "shared-sovereignty" with India, to greater autonomy within India, to the integration of all Naga-inhabited areas, to mere acknowledgement of Naga "uniqueness."

Criticisms, Caution, Critique

Notwithstanding its considerable success, the Forum for Naga Reconciliation has not been completely free from its critics on the questions of truth, justice, and the past. Long-lasting healing will never happen unless all the attitudes, values, and institutionalised justification that produced painful, sad and angry fallouts are acknowledged.

Nationalist Paramilitary Cadres Cleaning the Dimapur City Clock Tower (Photo by Kethoser Kevichusa, December 2009)

Nationalist Paramilitary Cadres Sporting "Naga Reconciliation" T-Shirts and Cleaning the Dimapur City Tower
(Photo by Kethoser Kevichusa, December 2009)

Nationalist Factions Greeting One Another During Pre-Christmas Reconciliation Meeting
(Photo by Kethoser Kevichusa, December 2009)

Forum for Naga Reconciliation Convenor Playing the Trumpet at Pre-Christmas Reconciliation Meeting
(Photo by Kethoser Kevichusa, December 2009)

Given this difficulty, the Forum for Naga Reconciliation, according to Wati, attempts what he calls a "win-win" proposal, both looking at the past but also looking to the future. Truth always involves interpretations, and looking into the past will not invariably lead to reconciliation. It can result in acrimonious blame-games that will only reopen old wounds and wrongs. Digging up the past can undermine the hard-won and fragile reconciliation process.

Nevertheless, there is little evidence that the Forum for Naga Reconciliation has, looked at the past; indeed, it's fixation on terms such has "journey", "destination", "hope", "future" gives the impression that they are more interested with the future than with the past.

It need not be that looking back into the past will necessarily end in acrimonious disputes and stall the reconciliation process. It is certainly possible to look into the past with sympathy and charity, while also making definite judgements about it. That, after all, is what forgiveness is all about. A shared future can be built by people who hold different views and interpretations about what happened in the past.

Sometimes blame has to be specifically apportioned. This does not necessarily mean that guilty individuals will have to be punished retributively, but it means that they have to take individual responsibility as and when necessary. There has to be a historical retrieval of some sort, and, when done, the Forum for Naga Reconciliation should call for acknowledgment of past wrongs.

The Forum for Naga Reconciliation and Expectations

The Forum for Naga Reconciliation should also be careful not to overly raise the expectations of the people. Most of the time, and especially at the complex political level, reconciliation remains frustratingly incomplete. It is more appropriately understood as a never-ending journey.

As a rule of thumb, the process of reconciliation takes at least as long as the period of the conflict itself. In the Naga context, this will mean that it will take decades rather than months or years. To predict that the reconciliation process could reach its destination within a couple of years would be unrealistic. Reconciliation takes time, and will take time, because it is a deep process. It involves profound changes in deep-seated emotions, attitudes, feelings, aspirations, and beliefs. Such changes cannot be imposed or rushed.

During the four years of the Forum for Naga Reconciliation, there has been a subtle but noticeable change in its discourse and rhetoric, as well as the issues that it broaches. What began as a call for an end to the factional killings and a call for reconciliation in the name of Jesus Christ has gradually moved to making serious political proposals.

The Forum for Naga Reconciliation must be extremely careful in making overtly political statements and proposals. This is not to say that it should not make any political proposal whatsoever. Any good political proposal coming from anywhere with regard to the Naga problem must be considered on its own merit. But there is a danger that making grand political proposals can be interpreted by different quarters in different ways, and can thus run the danger of losing credibility.

Other Questions

A major challenge for the Forum for Naga Reconciliation is that the Naga political problem remains unresolved. Here, Naga reconciliation is fundamentally different than most other reconciliation processes elsewhere. Processes of reconciliation, such as the Truth and Reconciliation Process in South Africa, are initiated *after* a political resolution. At the moment, it appears that "reconciliation" in Nagaland is taking primacy over "solution," and that the immediate goal of the reconciliation process seems to be for the different factions to "reconcile" and negotiate with India as a united front.

Another question that the reconciliation process raises is that of the criminal activities of the factions; according to a leading Naga businessman, there is a clear and direct correlation between reconciliation and extortion, the reason being that members of the different factions are able to move about more freely and safely. His conclusion, thus, was that reconciliation was not necessarily good for business activity!

Most people are of the view that the fragile work of the Forum for Naga Reconciliation should not be disturbed by other reconciliation initiatives. That was one of the reasons why the Naga Common Platform, a political reconciliation initiative of the Nagaland state government in 2009, was rejected by most of the Naga political groups, frontal organisations, and civil society groups.

When it comes to the greater question of "Naga reconciliation," the Forum for Naga Reconciliation and others must encourage multiple movements of forgiveness, peace, and reconciliation from various quarters. It seems to me that the burden of the reconciliation of a deeply divided society, such as the Naga society, cannot be borne by the Forum for Naga Reconciliation alone, and Nagas cannot afford to put all their reconciliation eggs in its basket.

Forgiveness in Politics and the Naga Conflict

Introduction

Forgiveness in the Naga political context will have to take place in the midst of a political conflict. In August 1957, two years after the beginning of the Indo-Naga conflict, when the first Naga People's Convention met, led by influential overground leaders, the outstanding resolution of that Convention was: "We maintain that the only answer to the Naga question is a satisfactory political settlement." During the Convention, a prominent moderate Naga leader, A. Kevichusa, also appealed to the hardliners: "My request to the underground leaders will be to be guided by the highest ideals of practical statesmanship." Eventually, however, it was the more hard-line, radical approach that won the day, leading to the Naga independence movement's fall into violence.

On the Indian side, the Naga demand for independence oscillated from acceptance to repression. Gandhi himself is reported to have said to a delegation of the NNC that the Nagas have every right to become independent. As the situation unravelled, it was, however, the hard-line approach of military repression taken by the

Government of India, combined with controversial dealings with certain sections of the Nagas, which epitomised India's approach to the Naga conflict.

More than five decades later, both the Naga nationalists and the Government of India are returning to direct political negotiations towards a resolution of their conflict. There are a number of reasons why the move from violence to non-violence, both at the Indo-Naga level and the intra-Naga level, can be interpreted as a form of forgiveness. To start, forgiveness is a term that is explicitly used as a basis for their talks and engagement in the reconciliation process. A statement made by top-level leaders of three different Naga factions in December 2011 says:

> *In the spirit of forgiveness we have agreed to let bygones be bygones and we are now prepared to understand each other and work for a shared Naga future. This does not mean there will not be any hurdles and difficulties before us. In fact the path to Naga Reconciliation is filled with many challenges. We believe that with the support and understanding of the people, we are certain to overcome all obstacles.*

What statements such as this make clear is that forgiveness is central to the process of politics in which the factions are now engaged. It is forgiveness which brings them to the dialogue and negotiation table. While the term *forgiveness* is not used at the Indo-Naga level, a move towards political negotiation between the nationalists and the Government of India can also be understood as a politics of forgiveness. There are a several reasons for this: it requires a measure of forbearance and engagement in dialogue with a view towards conciliation; it calls for a moderation and softening of deep resentments; it reflects a willingness to consider the enemy's perspective ; it calls for a resolve by all not to be determined by the wrongdoings of the past; and it reflects a realistic view of the existing political situation. There is also a sense in which the return to non-violent political activity on all sides can be interpreted as a kind of "repentance" – *metanoia* – a changing of minds and turning away from former violent methods to pursue their goals and positions.

This is not to minimise the complicated issues still standing in the way of a meaningful resolution of the Naga problem. For one, as the formal political talks between the Government of India and the Nagas is so far limited to only one nationalist group, other groups need to become part of the process.

Any resolution to the Naga conflict must also take into consideration the fact that non-Nagas – such as the Meiteis of Manipur, the Assamese of Assam, the non-Nagas of Arunachal Pradesh – are major stakeholders in the Indo-Naga issue. Any sort of integration of the Nagas within India under one territorial and administrative umbrella will require the re-drawing of state boundaries, which the neighbouring states have so far vehemently objected to. Here again, a politics of forgiveness will have to be employed in breaking the stalemate. Unless the interests of the neighbouring non-Nagas are also taken into consideration, any long-lasting peace in north-east India will not be possible. It is also in *their* interest that the Naga issue is resolved.

There are positive signs that reflect a thawing of the entrenched positions, both among the Naga political leaders and their counterparts in the neighbouring states. In an interview with *The Telegraph*, Neiphiu Rio, the pro-integration former Chief Minister of Nagaland said, "[W]ithout talking to them (Manipur) there can be no solution... We are living as neighbours, and we will continue to live as neighbours." The former Chief Minister of Manipur and the former Chief Minister of Assam have both expressed a wish to settle the conflict and live peacefully as good neighbours. These are positive, if fragile, signs that reflect a politics of forgiveness on the part of the Naga political leadership and their neighbouring counterparts.

A settlement that does not include the Nagas of Myanmar will also be incomplete. The redrawing of international borders to bring together all the Nagas under one political umbrella is, however, highly unlikely, at least in the foreseeable future. However, political developments in Myanmar can contribute in easing this sore point and the easing of tensions between the Naga nationalists and the Burmese government through the setting up of structures and policies that enable and sustain community building and friendship can itself be interpreted as a politics of forgiveness on the part of the Myanmar government and the Naga nationalists there.

Political Compromise

Endless political negotiations and dialogue are meaningless if they do not arrive at some sort of political settlement.

Striking a political deal will, however, call for compromise. On the part of the Naga nationalists, the biggest compromise is the issue of sovereignty. The current political leaders recognise the inevitability of making compromises on the two issues of sovereignty and integration, some speaking of shared sovereignty with India, and the Chief Minister of Nagaland, Neiphiu Rio, has called for the "emotional integration" of the Nagas, even if political and geographical integration is not possible.

Some nationalist groups will find compromise on sovereignty unacceptable, feeling that compromise would amount to a betrayal of the many thousands of lives that have been lost in the Indo-Naga conflict and that sovereignty is of greater worth than anything, including peace, development, and socio-economic stability.

Such objections against compromise are understandable, and have a great deal of emotive and rhetorical power. In responding to such an argument, it is important to note that a distinction needs to be made between those who died *for* or *fighting for* Naga independence, on the one hand, and those "bystanders" who died *because of* or *in the wake of* the conflict, on the other. With regard to the latter, the question to be asked is whether justice rather than sovereignty should be pursued. Indeed, it could also be said the struggle for Naga sovereignty should be discontinued precisely because too many Nagas have died and suffered *because of* and *in the wake of* the conflict.

Death is not the only way of honouring the dead: "He [Christ] died that we might live," is the logic of sacrifice not "He died so that we might also die". The death of the Naga martyrs is not a strong enough reason for committing present and future generations to carry on fighting unto death. To refuse to compromise solely on the grounds of keeping faith with the dead may be a genuine emotional impulse but it is not a reasonable proposition.

The objection that Nagas will not accept anything less than absolute sovereignty is also not true. There are sections among Nagas who are willing to make compromises on the issue of sovereignty. The hard-line nationalists are not the only Nagas nor the only voice of the Nagas; indeed, they are now the minority, and that the nationalist movement is no longer a "people's movement" as it was in the 1950s and 1960s. The great majority of Nagas now participate and vote voluntarily in the state and parliamentary elections, which are conducted under the purview of the Indian constitution. Nagas today compete for central and state government jobs and the Indian Republic Day and the Independence Day are celebrated peacefully in Nagaland.

Sovereignty and stability are neither mutually exclusive nor mutually inclusive. A nation can be both sovereign and at the same time be politically stable, peaceful, and economically developed. The willingness of the nationalists to make compromises on the question of sovereignty need not be taken to mean that they (or "the Naga people") have given up their belief and conviction about Naga sovereignty as such. Rather, it might simply be taken to mean that compromise on the issue is the only way of ensuring that the Naga people, who have for too long been caught in the vortex of violence, fear, and hatred, come to live with a measure of peace, freedom, and self-respect.

The rationale behind such an acceptance of a compromise can be interpreted as a politics of forgiveness for two basic reasons. Christian theology affirms that everything in the world is imperfect, including all existing political arrangements. Moreover, engaging with the existing political arrangements requires a politics of forgiveness. For Nagas, this will mean that they continue to engage with life under the Indian state, even if it is not their ideal situation.

It will also call for the forgiveness of the Naga nationalists who have, for the last several decades, caused immeasurable misery and loss to the Naga people. This forgiveness will lead to the possibility of a better and more peaceful future.

In recent years, a number of creative proposals for alternative arrangements for the Nagas have been put forward including the formation of a non-territorial Naga Regional Council that would not threaten nor affect the integrity of the other neighbouring states. Another proposal is the Saami model, whereby the Saami people living in the three different Scandinavian countries – Sweden, Finland, and Norway – have Saami parliaments, with limited power, provided by the constitutions of these countries.

The Nagas, along with the Indian government and the other neighbouring state governments, can work towards a council that will have power and jurisdiction, on certain agreed matters, over all the Nagas. While the core of the proposed Naga Council will be on cultural matters – such as marriage, inheritance, succession, local government, et cetera – the Council can give guidelines which must be respected by all the other states. This can give an integration to the Nagas without affecting the citizenship of the Nagas in India or the boundaries of the surrounding states.

A further model is a combination of the Saami Council model and the model of the indigenous people's institutions of Canada, which exercise increasing powers alongside provinces of Canada. Aspects of the Northern Ireland model could also be considered. Such a setup can acknowledge the legitimacy of the Nagas to self-determination, on the one hand, and the legitimacy of India, Burma, and the non-Naga neighbouring states to preserve and maintain their territorial integrity, on the other.

On 19th July 2012, the Joint Legislators Forum (JLF), comprising all the sixty members of the Nagaland Legislative Assembly agreed to look for any alternative arrangement that may come about from logical conclusion of the ongoing peace process.

Forgiveness and Justice in Nagaland

Notwithstanding all the talk of forgiveness and politics in Nagaland, the question of justice must not be ignored.

In Nagaland, a great deal of resentment, violence, and unforgiveness can be traced to the widespread culture of impunity, which make it politically and institutionally impossible for members of the Indian armed forces to be held accountable for the atrocities committed by them.

The ceasefire agreements between the powerful National Socialist Councils of Nagaland and the Government of India have also made it virtually impossible to arrest and detain, let alone incarcerate, members of these nationalist factions who are engaged in criminal activities, lest the peace process be jeopardised or derailed. Moreover, state government officials, the state police, and the political class are often fearful of these nationalist workers and seldom dare to attempt to bring these criminals to justice. In cases where arrests are made, judicial processes are prevented either through manipulation or brute force, which amount to what is called strategic or psychological impunity. In the absence of judicial redress, people not only resign themselves to existing political realities but also resort to private acts of vengeance, or live with deep-seated hatred of their enemies.

The problem of "whose justice" is also amply evident in the Naga conflict, where there is a volatile mix of de facto governments and a confusing assortment of laws and centres of power. What is *murder* to one family or factional group is *encounter killing* or *capital punishment* passed by the *court* of another group's *government* for *treason,* in the name of *justice*. What is draconian according to one party is reasonable according to another. The point being made here is that, in conflict situations such as the Naga conflict, competing accounts of justice lock conflicting parties into tortuous stalemates, while societies continue to languish in violence.

In the Naga context, it is extremely important that the language, vocabulary, and practice of justice progress simultaneously with the on-going peace and reconciliation processes. It will be limited and imperfect. This limitation has to do with the impossibility of clear discrimination between the guilty and the innocent. The "knotted histories" of individuals, groups, tribes, cultures, and races, make the disentangling of the innocent from the blameworthy more difficult and complex than they initially appear.

It is not desirable to have one grand "official" interpretation of the Naga political past. It also must not be assumed that knowledge of the truth will be a sufficient condition for forgiveness and reconciliation. In most cases, people often already know who is responsible for the killing of their loved ones.

If it is unrealistic to expect consensus regarding the Naga political past, the same holds with regard to the Naga political future.

Different groups, whether they be the Indian government, the present state government of Nagaland, the nationalist groups, and others, all have different hopes and fears, in different political arrangements. The Naga political future will also remain contested.

Yet, it certainly is possible for there to be a measure of consensus on some aspects of the past and the future. While it could be argued that the violence meted out against the Nagas by India was from the beginning an intentional, systematic programme of violent imperialism, a more sympathetic and empathetic perspective could also be taken. India, in the early years after independence, was a perilously volatile and fledgling nation that had had no respite from its pre-independence turmoil and uncertainty. It was unequipped for the turbulent problems and challenges facing it after independence – a bloody partition and the staggering levels of migrations and violence that followed, a war with Pakistan over Kashmir, the internal threats of independence from various regions and princely states, the massive challenges of statecraft and nation-building. When some of these problems that India faced are taken into consideration in a charitable spirit, it is perhaps understandable that the Government of India reacted to the Naga problem with the violent and repressive measures that it did. After all, theirs was a new-born republic, and their people faced the enormous task of bringing stability to a nation tackling the problems of the Partition.

Yet, the Government of India can take certain steps towards some form of justice, by recognition. This would require an honest acknowledgement on the part of India that it is partly responsible for the conflict, and that there have been excesses on its part. Along with recognition, there can be *reparation.* There are, no doubt, a number of important questions and complex modalities that need to be raised and dealt with in regard to reparation. Assuming that the Government of India is forthcoming with reparations, a plan can be worked out with stakeholders, both on the Indian and the Naga side.

With some of the most prominent Naga nationalist groups now around the negotiation table, and increasingly showing a willingness to make compromises on the independence issue, an act of reparation can contribute to trust-building and peace-building between Nagas and India, which, in turn, can lead to a more politically stable and economically prosperous north-east. A courageous display of such political statesmanship can also contribute to India's moral and political standing in the international community as a mature and responsible democracy. It will also convey and reinforce the oft-repeated message to the Nagas by India that they are fully equal citizens of the Indian state, with equal dignity, protection, and self-esteem.

But the reparation must also be "reasonable" in the sense that such a reparation programme will neither prove too costly nor come too cheaply, especially if such a reparation programme is going to be in monetary form. One of the main reasons why many an international- or national-level reparation programme stalls is the financial burden on the exchequer. If the financial costs prove too high, then taxpaying citizens, most of whom may be generations removed from the actual historical events, can be resistant to it. And yet, at the same time, such a reparation programme must not come cheap financially. If it is, it will only create further resentment.

To that extent, a reparation programme must also be sensitive psychologically and culturally to the potential recipients and contributors. It must also be symbolic, emphasising the reparative nature of the programme; to that extent, it must be distinct from other governmental programmes and activities aimed at infrastructure and socio-economic development. It must also discriminate between the collective and individual. There is a sense in which all the Nagas have suffered, and are, to that extent, entitled to reparation. But it is also true that some individuals and families have suffered more directly and terribly under Indian army atrocities through torture, killings, rape, and disappearances.

Besides recognition and reparation, a third thing that the GOI can do is *retraction*. In particular, the Government of India can withdraw the Armed Forces (Special Powers) Act from the Naga areas. Since 1958, this Act has been in place in the Naga areas and is responsible for much army brutality and concomitant Naga resentment against India. If part of justice includes the disabling of wrongdoers, then the withdrawal of the AFSPA can be meaningfully interpreted as a form of justice which disables the Indian military forces operating in the Naga areas. Given also the fact that the Naga nationalists have all made it more or less clear that they will not be going to war against India.

With respect to the nationalist wrongdoers, three things could be done which would reflect a measure of justice. Firstly, there can be a disabling of wrongdoers. An important purpose of justice and punishment is the protection of victims (and would-be victims), which often takes this form of disabling wrongdoers. In Northern Ireland, one of the main factors that contributed to the peace process and the stable peace that has ensued since the Good Friday Agreement is the complete and irreversible decommissioning of weapons. It seems to me that the Forum for Naga Reconciliation can also make a call to the factions along similar lines. It should seize upon an opportunity to call for a complete decommissioning of arms.

This will disable wrongdoers and make them injure no more; it will rid Nagaland of thousands of dangerous weapons and thereby contribute to the safety of the people; it will enable the general Naga populace to have a level of confidence and trust in the new political dispensation; and it may encourage the other nationalist groups to also lay down their arms.

A second thing that can be done is the erection of a public memorial accorded to the dead, where rituals of commemoration can be made, as a symbol of justice, to help assuage the resentment of the bereaved on all sides by according their dead relatives a certain respect and dignity. One creative proposal for collective healing and reconciliation in Naga society was made in 2003 by the Naga Peoples Movement for Human Rights (NPMHR), as part of their twenty-fifth commemoration. The proposal was titled *A Naga Forest of Remembrance* and suggested planting one tree for every precious life. Unfortunately, the project did not materialise. This could be revisited and could form a place of reconciliation.

It would be very difficult for the different sides to commemorate the dead of the opposing sides. But one can commemorate the dead without necessarily implying that one approves of what they stood for or what they did. To commemorate and even to commiserate, one does not need to agree with the cause for which the fallen died.

Another dimension of justice is for a place or platform for public truth-telling, where the voices of both political victims and perpetrators can be heard. (Such a model could be similar but not necessarily the same as South Africa's TRC.) This accords the victims the dignity of their voices being heard and their pain being shared, creates a space for wrongdoers from any side to acknowledge their wrongdoing, and it can be an expression of the dignity of the Naga people – a people who take wrongdoing in their midst seriously, care for their victims thoughtfully, and forgive wrongdoers charitably.

Conclusion

Forgiveness and politics have an intimate relationship. Forgiveness, far from being inimical to politics, is an inherently political concept and practice, and politics is itself a forgiving enterprise.

The most helpful approach for a biblically based Christian understanding and practice of forgiveness must pay attention to the metanarrative of the Bible that stretches from the creation to the new creation and presents the vision of a world that is created but fallen, fallen but redeemed, redeemed but not fully redeemed. With this in view, one is able to appreciate how forgiveness becomes a mode of engagement with the whole of reality and, as presented by the Bible, is both a divine and human response. It also makes forgiveness not merely an interpersonal response, but a response to the whole of the reality. The distinct markers of metanarrative of the Bible (Creation, Covenant, Christ, Church, and Consummation) also have immense potential in illuminating and informing the understanding and practice of forgiveness, making forgiveness not just a religious or personal concept and practice, but also a political one.

In exploring the concept of politics, some of the most salient features of political activity cannot be sustained or practiced without forgiveness, and politics is itself an inherently a forgiving enterprise.

There are certain promising proposals for relating forgiveness and justice. Justice, both primary and rectifying justice, can be understood as intrinsically related to forgiveness, and an understanding of justice as *epieikeia* is a form of justice that tends toward forgiveness. Within such a conception of justice, the practice and purpose of punishment, which includes expression, affirmation, vindication, instruction, and reconciliation, is not in conflict with forgiveness. Understood in this sense, the tension between forgiveness and politics, based on the objection that it conflicts with justice can be significantly relaxed.

Reconciliation can also be understood as a political concept and practice. Forgiveness animates and undergirds the elements that are considered essential for reconciliation in societies mired in political conflict. These elements include mercy, truth, justice, and peace; if these elements are essential to reconciliation in divided political entities, then forgiveness is itself essential for reconciliation because these elements cannot be understood or realised without factoring in the concept and practice of forgiveness.

In Northern Ireland, there have been many instances of apology and forgiveness coming from individuals, religious leaders, and political actors, but it is the political process leading up to and culminating in the Good Friday Agreement of 1998 that presents the most hopeful case of forgiveness in politics within the Northern Ireland conflict. The Good Friday Agreement of 1998 is usually not taken as an instance of forgiveness in politics, but it does meet, if imperfectly, the demands of justice in Northern Ireland and forgiveness creates the space for political activity that breaks the cycle of violence.

Forgiveness in politics in Nagaland today can be best understood by looking at the move of the Naga nationalists from violence to negotiated politics, both at the Indo-Naga conflict and the intra-Naga conflict levels. There are a number of difficulties that stand in the way of a political settlement of the Indo-Naga problem. However, while forgiveness may not be a be-all and end-all, any process towards a resolution and conciliation of the various conflicting interests and perspectives must employ a politics of forgiveness. Compromise on the question of Naga independence is inevitable, and will itself require a politics of forgiveness.

The question of justice must not be ignored in Nagaland and a number of recommendations can be made which are compatible with forgiveness in politics, and can be taken in a way that does not jeopardise the fragile peace and reconciliation process but promotes peace and reconciliation in Nagaland today.

Despite the limitations in the scope of this book and the more comprehensive thesis from which it is derived, the author has endeavoured to show that forgiveness and politics are related. Furthermore, I would venture to claim that forgiveness is an appropriate shorthand for the whole process of "reasoning together" that politics is all about, and that the Scriptures themselves point to:

> *"Come now, and let us reason together," says the LORD. "Though your sins are like scarlet, they shall be as white as snow; though they are red like crimson, they shall be like wool." (Isa. 1:18, NKJV)*

Appendix
Declaration of Support for the Good Friday Agreement

1. We, the participants in the multi-party negotiations, believe that the agreement we have negotiated offers a truly historic opportunity for a new beginning.
2. The tragedies of the past have left a deep and profoundly regrettable legacy of suffering. We must never forget those who have died or been injured, and their families. But we can best honour them through a fresh start, in which we firmly dedicate ourselves to the achievement of reconciliation, tolerance, and mutual trust, and to the protection and vindication of the human rights of all.
3. We are committed to partnership, equality and mutual respect as the basis of relationships within Northern Ireland, between North and South, and between these islands.
4. We reaffirm our total and absolute commitment to exclusively democratic and peaceful means of resolving differences on political issues, and our opposition to any use or threat of force by others for any political purpose, whether in regard to this agreement or otherwise.

5. We acknowledge the substantial differences between our continuing, and equally legitimate, political aspirations. However, we will endeavour to strive in every practical way towards reconciliation and rapprochement within the framework of democratic and agreed arrangements. We pledge that we will, in good faith, work to ensure the success of each and every one of the arrangements to be established under this agreement. It is accepted that all of the institutional and constitutional arrangements – an Assembly in Northern Ireland, a North/South Ministerial Council, implementation bodies, a British-Irish Council and a British-Irish Intergovernmental Conference and any amendments to British Acts of Parliament and the Constitution of Ireland – are interlocking and interdependent and that in particular the functioning of the Assembly and the North/South Council are so closely inter-related that the success of each depends on that of the other.
6. Accordingly, in a spirit of concord, we strongly commend this agreement to the people, North and South, for their approval.

Bibliography

Adams, Gerry. *The Politics of Irish Freedom* Dingle: Brandon Books, 1986.

Amstutz, Mark. *The Healing of Nations: The Promise and Limits of Political Forgiveness* Lanham, MD: Rowman & Littlefield, 2005.

Biggar, Nigel. "Forgiving Enemies in Ireland", *Journal of Religious Ethics* 36, no. 4, (2008), pp. 559-79.

——— *Burying the Past: Making Peace and Doing Justice after Civil Conflict* Expanded and Updated edn; Washington, DC: Georgetown University Press, 2003.

——— "Peace and Justice: A Limited Reconciliation", *Ethical Theory and Moral Practice* 5, (June 2002), pp. 167-79.

Chasie, Charles. *The Naga Imbroglio: A Personal Perspective* Kohima: Standard Printers and Publishers, 1999.

Daly, "Reflections on How Forgiveness Has Functioned in Northern Ireland (a Catholic View)" in *Woodstock Colloquium Forgiveness in Conflict Resolution: Reality and Utility – The Northern Ireland*

Experience Washington, DC: Woodstock Theological Center, Georgetown University, 1997.

Kerr, Cecil. *The Way of Peace* London: Hodder & Stoughton, 1990.

Lederach, John Paul. *Building Peace: Sustainable Reconciliation in Divided Societies* Washington, D.C.: United States Institute of Peace Press, 1997 [2006].

Linyü, Keviyiekielie. *Christian Movements in Nagaland* Kohima: N.V. Press, 2004.

Mallie, Eamon and David McKittrick. *Endgame in Ireland* London: Hodder & Stoughton, 2001.

Mitchell, Claire. *Religion, Identity and Politics in Northern Ireland: Boundaries of Belonging and Belief* Aldershot: Ashgate, 2006.

Nussbaum, Martha. "Equity and Mercy," *Philosophy and Public Affairs* 22, no. 2 (1993), pp 83-125.

O'Donovan, Oliver. *The Ways of Judgment* Grand Rapids, MI: Eerdmans, 2005.

——— *Resurrection and Moral Order* Second edn; Leicester: InterVarsity Press, 1986 [1994].

——— *Measure for Measure: Justice in Punishment and the Sentence of Death* Bramcote: Grove Books, 1977.

O'Higgins, Kevin. "The Courts and Forgiveness" in *Remembering to Forgive: A Tribute to Una O'Higgins O'Malley*, ed. Enda McDonagh. Dublin: Veritas Publications, 2007.

O'Neill, Joseph R. *The Irish Potato Famine* Edina, MN: ABDO Publishing Company, 2009.

Pope John Paul II, *No Peace without Justice, No Justice without Forgiveness: Message of His Holiness Pope John Paul II for the Celebration of the World Day of Peace.* 1st January 2002.

Powell, Jonathan. *Great Hatred, Little Room: Making Peace in Northern Ireland* London: Vintage, 2009.

Ruane, Joseph and Jennifer Todd. *The Dynamics of Conflict in Northern Ireland: Power, Conflict and Emancipation* Cambridge: Cambridge University Press, 1996.

Vanhoozer, Kevin J. *The Drama of Doctrine: A Canonical Linguistic Approach to Christian Theology* Louisville, KY: Westminster John Knox Press, 2005.

Williams, Rowan. "The Suspicion of Suspicion: Wittgenstein and Bonnhoeffer" in *The Grammar of the Heart*, ed. Richard H. Bell. San Francisco: Harper and Row, 1988.

Willmer, Haddon. "The Politics of Forgiveness: A New Dynamic," *The Furrow* 30, no. 4 (1979), pp. 207-218.

——— "Forgiveness and Politics," *Crucible*, July-September, (1979).

Wright, N. T. *New Testament and the People of God* London: SPCK, 1992 [2004].

End Notes

[1] Kevin J. Vanhoozer, *The Drama of Doctrine: A Canonical Linguistic Approach to Christian Theology* (Louisville, KY: Westminster John Knox Press, 2005), p. 315.

[2] N. T. Wright, *New Testament and the People of God* (London: SPCK, 1992 [2004]).

[3] Oliver O'Donovan, *Resurrection and Moral Order* (Second edn; Leicester: InterVarsity Press, 1986 [1994]), p. 55.

[4] Oliver O'Donovan, *The Ways of Judgment* (Grand Rapids, MI: Eerdmans, 2005), p. 100.

[5] Haddon Willmer, "The Politics of Forgiveness: A New Dynamic," *The Furrow* 30, no. 4 (1979).

[6] Oliver O'Donovan, *Measure for Measure: Justice in Punishment and the Sentence of Death* (Bramcote: Grove Books, 1977), p. 9.

[7] Kevin O'Higgins, "The Courts and Forgiveness" in *Remembering to Forgive: A Tribute to Una O'Higgins O'Malley*, ed. Enda McDonagh (Dublin: Veritas Publications, 2007).

[8] Oliver O'Donovan, *Measure for Measure: Justice in Punishment and the Sentence of Death* (Bramcote: Grove Books, 1977), p. 9.

[9] Oliver O'Donovan, *The Ways of Judgment* (Grand Rapids, MI: Eerdmans, 2005), p. 19.

[10] Pope John Paul II, *No Peace without Justice, No Justice without Forgiveness: Message of His Holiness Pope John Paul II for the Celebration of the World Day of Peace* (1st January 2002).

[11] Martha Nussbaum, "Equity and Mercy," *Philosophy and Public Affairs* 22, no. 2 (1993).

[12] Haddon Willmer, "Forgiveness and Politics," *Crucible,* July-September, (1979), p. 101.

[13] Nigel Biggar, *Burying the Past: Making Peace and Doing Justice after Civil Conflict* (Expanded and Updated edn; Washington, DC: Georgetown University Press, 2003), p. 312.

[14] Rowan Williams, "The Suspicion of Suspicion: Wittgenstein and Bonnhoeffer" in *The Grammar of the Heart*, ed. Richard H. Bell (San Francisco: Harper and Row, 1988), p. 44.

[15] <https://www.sahistory.org.za/archive/kairos-document-theological-comment-political-crisis-south-africa> [accessed 3rd February 2021].

[16] In Northern Ireland, there are many IRAs: the "Original IRA" or "Old IRA" (OIRA) which split after the 1921 Treaty into pro-Treaty and the anti-Treaty groups; the IRA (1922-1969), which was the anti-Treaty group before it split in 1969 into the "Official IRA" (OIRA) and the "Provisional IRA" (PIRA); the "Continuity IRA" (CIRA) which split from PIRA in 1986; the "Real IRA" (RIRA) which split from the PIRA in 1997.

[17] Claire Mitchell, *Religion, Identity and Politics in Northern Ireland: Boundaries of Belonging and Belief* (Aldershot: Ashgate, 2006), p. 3.

[18] Gerry Adams, *The Politics of Irish Freedom* (Dingle: Brandon Books, 1986), p. 89.

[19] Joseph Ruane and Jennifer Todd, *The Dynamics of Conflict in Northern Ireland: Power, Conflict and Emancipation* (Cambridge: Cambridge University Press, 1996).

[20] Cecil Kerr, *The Way of Peace* (London: Hodder & Stoughton, 1990), pp. 173-174.

[21] Cited in Daly, "Reflections on How Forgiveness Has Functioned in Northern Ireland (a Catholic View)" in *Woodstock Colloquium Forgiveness in Conflict Resolution: Reality and Utility – The Northern Ireland Experience* (Washington, DC: Woodstock Theological Center, Georgetown University, 1997), p. 5.

[22] Daly, "Reflections," pp. 5-6.

[23] Joseph R. O'Neill, *The Irish Potato Famine* (Edina, MN: ABDO Publishing Company, 2009), p. 12.

[24] Mark Amstutz, *The Healing of Nations: The Promise and Limits of Political Forgiveness* (Lanham, MD: Rowman & Littlefield, 2005), p. 179.

[25] Eamon Mallie and David McKittrick, *Endgame in Ireland* (London: Hodder & Stoughton, 2001), p. 81.

[26] Jonathan Powell, *Great Hatred, Little Room: Making Peace in Northern Ireland* (London: Vintage, 2009), p. 313.

[27] Nigel Biggar, "Forgiving Enemies in Ireland", *Journal of Religious Ethics* 36, no. 4, (2008), pp. 559-79.

[28] Nigel Biggar, "Peace and Justice: A Limited Reconciliation", *Ethical Theory and Moral Practice* 5, (June 2002), pp. 167-79.

[29] To be sure, since the completion of my thesis in 2013, there have been some developments in the Naga political conflict and process. But since these developments do not, in my judgment, significantly contradict or detract from the central analyses and arguments that the thesis made in 2013, they are being reproduced (albeit in abridged form) as they were written back then. The content is also being reproduced as it was written then in order to preserve the integrity of the original work.

[30] Keviyiekielie Linyü, *Christian Movements in Nagaland* (Kohima: N.V. Press, 2004), p. 149.

[31] Charles Chasie, *The Naga Imbroglio: A Personal Perspective* (Kohima: Standard Printers and Publishers, 1999), p. 43.

[32] John Paul Lederach, *Building Peace: Sustainable Reconciliation in Divided Societies* (Washington, D.C.: United States Institute of Peace Press, 1997 [2006]).